ANIMALS

INCREDIBLE BUT TRUE FACTS

This edition published by Parragon Books Ltd in 2015

Parragon Books Ltd
Chartist House
15–17 Trim Street
Bath BA1 1HA, UK
www.parragon.com

Copyright © Parragon Books Ltd 2007-2015

Written by Sally Morgan
Consultants: Mandy Holloway and Gerald Legg

ISBN 978-1-4748-1411-9

Printed in China

ANIMALS

INCREDIBLE BUT TRUE FACTS

PaRragon

Bath • New York • Cologne • Melbourne • Delhi
Hong Kong • Shenzhen • Singapore • Amsterdam

CONTENTS

Introduction 6

The animal kingdom 8

Living on land 28

Living in the air 106

Living in water 130

Index 172

Introduction

Animals are found in every part of the world, from the warm rainforests to the freezing Poles, and from high mountains to the deepest oceans.

This book tells you all about the amazing world of animals. You can read about the many different places where animals live, and find out how animals survive in their surroundings. You can also learn about the large number of animals that are under threat and what we can do to help them.

THE ANIMAL KINGDOM

There are more than one and a half million different types, or species, of animal in the world – and there are millions more still waiting to be discovered. Animals come in many different shapes, sizes and colours. They live in lots of different places and behave in very different ways. The largest animal is the gigantic blue whale, but some animals are as small as tiny specks of dust.

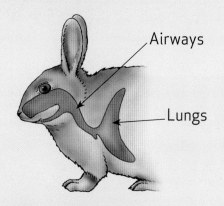

Airways

Lungs

Animal Features

Animals may look very different, but they are alike in many ways. They all breathe, feed and grow. Most animals have senses so that they can see, smell, hear, taste and touch what is around them.

Breathing

Many animals breathe using lungs. When this rabbit breathes in, it pulls air down its airways into its lungs.

Feeding

Plants can make their own food but animals have to find something to eat. Animals that feed on plants are called herbivores. Animals that eat other animals are called carnivores.

This heron is a carnivore and it feeds on smaller animals such as fish.

Moving around

Animals move in different ways. They walk on land, fly in the air or swim in water. Animals move to find food, to escape from a hunter or to find a partner.

Did you know?

The Atlantic giant squid has the largest eyes in the world. Each eyeball measures 40 centimetres across.

Fish use fins to steer in the water.

Raising young

Animals have many different ways of having babies. Some give birth to live young, while others, such as birds and reptiles, lay eggs from which the young hatch.

The senses

Animals use their senses of sight, hearing, smell, taste and touch to hunt for food, defend themselves and to detect the world around them. For example, owls have large eyes, which they use to hunt for prey at night.

Body Parts

Animals can be divided into two groups. One group of animals has a backbone, which is like a stiff rod running down the back of the body. These animals are called vertebrates. The other group is the invertebrates – these animals do not have backbones.

Skull

These bones are from the skeleton of a bird.

Skeletons

Fish, amphibians, reptiles, birds and mammals are all vertebrates. Their bones make up the skeleton. The skeleton supports the animal's body and the muscles that are used to move about.

Jellyfish

Jellyfish are invertebrates that live in water. Water supports their body, so when they are out of it, jellyfish collapse into a wobbly mass of jelly.

Protected by a shell

A snail is an invertebrate. It has a shell that protects its soft body. The snail moves along using its large foot.

A snail's foot runs along the bottom of its body.

Tough armour

Crabs are invertebrates and belong to a group of animals called arthropods. Arthropods are protected by a tough outer covering called an external skeleton. Other arthropods include insects, spiders and centipedes.

Backbone

Brain

Heart

Lungs

Liver

Stomach

Intestines

Body organs

An organ is a part of an animal's body that has a particular job to do. For example, the eyes are used to see and the heart pumps the blood around the body. Like other animals, the human body contains many different organs, including the heart, lungs, liver and brain.

Animal Behaviour

Everything that an animal does is part of its behaviour. Some behaviour has to be learned, either by watching a parent or by the animal trying something for itself.

Communicating with sound

Many animals use sound to communicate with each other. An animal, such as a lion or a wolf, may use sound to tell its rivals to stay away or to attract a partner.

Wolves howl to communicate with each other.

Using colour

Some animals use bright colours to attract a partner. Male peacocks have brightly coloured tail feathers, which they raise to form fans. Females choose the males that make the best display.

Learning behaviour

Chimpanzees have learned how to use simple tools. They push long sticks into termite nests. The termites grip the sticks, then the chimpanzees pull the sticks out and eat the termites.

Hunting

Lion cubs learn how to hunt by watching their mothers. By the time they are a couple of years old, the cubs are ready to hunt on their own.

Living together

Animals that live in large groups can hunt together and protect each other. Many fish swim in large groups called shoals. All the fish within a shoal swim together, moving as if they were one.

Life Cycles

Animals give birth or lay eggs to produce young animals. This is called reproduction. These young animals grow up, have young of their own and then die. This is known as a life cycle.

Amphibians

Toads belong to a group of animals called amphibians. They lay a mass of tiny black eggs, called frogspawn, in water. Each egg is covered in jelly.

Did you know?

The oldest animal ever recorded was an Icelandic cyprine, which is a type of shellfish. One example lived for 374 years.

Birds

Birds lay eggs. The eggs have to be kept warm while the chicks grow inside. When a chick is ready to hatch, it uses a special tooth on the end of its beak to break out of its shell.

Budding hydras

The hydra is a simple animal that lives in water. A hydra reproduces by growing a new, identical hydra in a method called budding. A bud appears on the side of the hydra's body. This bud grows and drops off to form a new hydra.

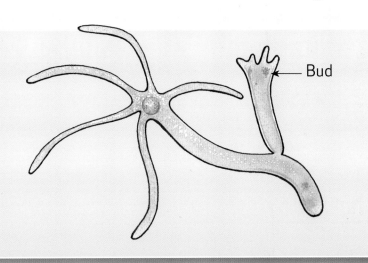

Bud

Feeding on milk

Mammals give birth to live young. After the babies are born, mammals feed their young with milk made by the mothers.

Sheep are mammals that feed milk to their young.

A long life

Some animals live for just a few days, while others will live for many years. Elephants, for example, grow very slowly and live for a long time. Some live to 80 years of age.

Animal Habitats

The place where an animal lives is called its habitat. A habitat is made up of a community, or group, of plants and animals. There are many different types of habitat, such as mountains, seas and cities.

The sea

The sea is the world's biggest habitat. There are deep oceans as well as shallow stretches of water near to land. Animals that are found in the sea are adapted to living in salty water.

Living on mountains

Conditions on mountains change with the height. Near the peaks, it is cold and windy. Few animals live here. Lower down, there are meadows and forests, where most of the animals live.

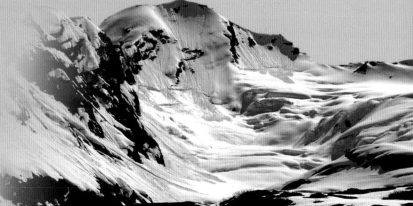

Living in cities

Many animals have moved into towns and cities. Birds nest in trees in parks and in buildings, while hedgehogs and foxes visit gardens and parks.

Freshwater life

Lakes and rivers are home to many different kinds of animal. These animals are used to living in fresh water, which is water that contains very little or no salt. They include frogs, fish and pond snails.

A pile of logs offers animals lots of dark places to live.

Forest homes

Woods and forests are full of trees. These offer animals lots of places to make a home and plenty of food to eat. Even a pile of logs is home to many different animals, such as slugs, centipedes and woodlice, as well as mice and snakes.

Food Chains

All animals rely on other living things for food. Some animals eat plants, such as grass, while others hunt the plant-eating animals. This is called a food chain.

Plants

Plants are able to make their own food. They take energy from sunlight and use it to make food. They store this food in their leaves. This means that plants are full of good things for plant-eating animals to eat.

Animals that only eat plants, such as antelopes, are called herbivores.

Plant eaters

The plant eaters are the first animals in the food chain. On the African plains, for example, large herds of antelopes eat grass, while giraffes eat the leaves off trees.

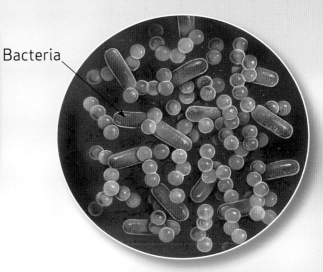

Bacteria

Did you know?

Bacteria are so small that more than one million of them could fit onto the head of a pin.

Meat eaters

The plant eaters are hunted by the meat eaters, or carnivores. Lions and leopards are carnivores that hunt antelopes and other grazing animals.

Recycling the waste

Bacteria break down the remains of dead animals. They recycle the bodies back into the soil to be used by plants.

Animals that hunt, such as leopards, are called predators.

Nature at Risk

Sometimes, habitats are damaged by natural events, such as a drought or a fire. However, a lot of damage is caused by people. Forests are cut down, grassland is ploughed up and harmful substances are pumped into the ground, air, rivers and oceans.

Clearing trees

Each year, millions of trees in forests are cut down. Sometimes, this is to clear the land for farming or housing. This destroys animals' homes as well as the food they eat.

Too many fish

When fishermen catch too many fish in their nets, animals such as seals, sea birds, whales and dolphins starve and the fish population is destroyed.

Oil spills

Large ships called tankers carry oil around the world. Occasionally, the tankers have accidents and oil spills into the sea. The oil kills sea birds and other animals.

Sea birds that are covered in oil cannot float and they quickly drown.

Did you know?

The world's rainforests are being cut down so quickly that they could disappear completely in just 45 years.

Global warming can damage habitats and kill animals that cannot survive in the new conditions.

Climate change

When fuels are burned, they release gases into the atmosphere. These gases are thought to be changing the Earth's climate and making temperatures hotter. This is called global warming.

Extinct is Forever

Animals become extinct (die out) for many reasons, such as a change in their habitat. For example, if the climate gets warmer, the animal may not survive this change.

Ancient animals

Crocodiles are ancient animals that were around when dinosaurs roamed the Earth. Unlike the dinosaurs, crocodiles have survived. Other ancient animals include alligators and tortoises.

Dinosaurs, such as *Tyrannosaurus rex*, could not survive in the new climate.

Reptile relics

Dinosaurs disappeared 65 million years ago. They became extinct because the world's climate changed. The dinosaurs could not survive this change, so they died out.

Hunted to death

Dodos were a kind of flightless bird that lived on the island of Mauritius in the Indian Ocean. They became extinct in the 1600s because they were hunted by humans.

Did you know?

In 2012, the World Conservation Union published a list of 19,817 animals, plants and fungi that may become extinct.

Under threat

Many well-known animals could become extinct in the next 10 years or so, including the giant panda, tiger and black rhino. A few of these animals survive in national parks and zoos, where they are protected.

Conserving Animals

The best way to save endangered animals is to conserve, or protect, their habitats. This can be done by creating national parks and by adopting sustainable farming practices.

Bird watching

People can watch animals in protected areas. This building is called a hide, and people use it to watch birds without disturbing them.

Watching animals

Some African countries, such as South Africa and Tanzania, have turned large areas into game reserves and national parks. Animals that live inside these areas are protected from pollution and human hunters.

Many tourists visit game reserves and national parks to watch the animals.

Did you know?

The world's first national park was Yellowstone National Park in the United States, created in 1872.

Cleaning up

Everybody can help to protect animal habitats. Rubbish can be harmful to animals, so these people are clearing it from a pond.

Organic farming

Many farmers use chemicals called pesticides and fertilizers to grow their crops. These chemicals can harm wildlife. Organic farming is a way of farming that does not use these chemicals, so wild animals are not harmed.

These pigs on an organic farm are free range, which means they are allowed to walk outside.

LIVING ON LAND

There are many different habitats on land. Forests have lots of trees growing closely together. Grasslands have lots of grasses and very few trees. Deserts are the driest places in the world, while the Poles at the top and bottom of the world are the coldest habitats.

Rainforests

Tropical rainforests are amazing places. They are found in the hot and wet parts of the world, close to the Equator, the region around the middle of the Earth. The trees grow close together and very little light reaches the forest floor.

Roof over the forest

The tops of the trees form a canopy – the 'roof' of the rainforest. The canopy may be 25 to 40 metres above the ground.

Boas coil themselves around the branches of trees when they are resting.

Did you know?

More than half the world's animals live in the rainforests. There are many more kinds of animal waiting to be discovered in these forests.

Hunting in trees

The boa is just one of many kinds of snake that can be found living in the canopy. Pythons lie hidden in the branches, waiting for their prey to pass.

The forest floor

Few plants are found growing on the forest floor. This is because it is too dark. The ground is covered with a layer of fallen leaves and fruit.

Roots in the air

Some plants do not grow in the soil. Instead, they grow on other plants, with their roots dangling in the air. These plants are called epiphytes. Some epiphytes produce colourful flowers that attract birds and insects.

Inside a rainforest

The plants in a rainforest grow in four layers. A few of the tallest trees poke through the rainforest canopy. Just beneath the canopy are smaller trees and shrubs. Finally, at the very bottom, is the dark forest floor.

Tallest trees

Canopy

Smaller trees and shrubs

Floor

Life in the Canopy

Most of the rainforest animals live in the canopy. They have learned how to move from tree to tree and where to find food and water. Some animals never come down to the ground.

Orange ape

Orang-utans have long arms and legs. Their fingers are hooked to help them grip branches as they climb through the trees looking for fruit.

Did you know?

Although most chameleons eat insects, a few species are big enough to catch and eat birds.

Colourful beak

The toucan eats fruit. It uses its long beak to reach fruit that grows at the ends of small branches.

This katydid is coloured green so that it can hide among the leaves.

Insects in the canopy

Many different kinds of insect are found in the canopy, where they eat leaves. These insects may be eaten by larger animals, such as birds or lizards.

Tough beak

The scarlet macaw has a powerful hooked beak. It uses this to crack open nuts and as an extra claw to climb up the trunks of trees.

Chameleons catch insects to eat using their very long tongues.

Clever camouflage

Chameleons can change the colour of their skin so that they blend in with the leaves of the trees. This is called camouflage and it makes the animals difficult to spot.

Keeping in Touch

Rainforests are noisy places. The trees block out much of the sunlight, so it is quite gloomy. This makes it hard for animals to see each other, so they talk to each other instead.

Cicadas make a noise by vibrating thin, drum-like pieces of skin on their bodies.

Noisy cicadas

Cicadas are insects that make a deafening sound! They make these sounds when the weather changes, when they are about to mate or if they have been disturbed.

Howling monkeys

The howler monkey is the world's loudest land-living animal. Its booming call carries for up to 5 kilometres through the forest.

Frog chorus

Most rainforest frogs are active
at night. This is when their
croaking can be heard. The
male frogs croak to
attract female frogs.

When one red-eyed tree
frog starts to croak, all
the nearby frogs start
croaking to create a
deafening chorus.

Bird song

Birds sing for many
reasons. Some sing to tell
other birds to stay away, while
others sing to attract a partner.
Each kind of bird has its own song.
The cockatoo makes screeching
and whistling sounds.

Moving Around

Rainforest animals have many ways of moving around the canopy. Some run along branches and jump from tree to tree. Others swing from branch to branch using their arms and tails.

Slow mover

Sloths move so slowly in the branches that moss and algae grow on their fur. This makes sloths slightly green in colour and helps them to hide in the trees.

A spider monkey's tail is so strong that it can support the monkey's weight.

Gripping tail

The spider monkey has a long tail, which it uses just like an extra leg. The monkey can wrap its tail around branches, using it to swing through the trees easily.

Did you know?

Sloths spend most of their time hanging upside down from branches. They sleep for 15 hours every day.

Gibbons swing
from one arm
to the other.

Swinging around

Animals such as gibbons and spider monkeys can
swing through the trees because they have very
flexible shoulders. Swinging is a very fast way of
getting around, and the animals can move through
trees faster than a human can walk on the ground.

Slithering snakes

Snakes move from one branch
to another by stretching out their
heads and holding on with their tails. They
slither through the branches looking for birds,
reptiles and mammals to eat.

Rainforest Floor

The rainforest floor is dark and damp. Much of it is covered in leaves, twigs and fruit that have fallen from the trees. Few plants can survive in the gloom.

Tapirs

Tapirs are some of the largest animals that live on the forest floor. They are pig-like animals with long, rubbery noses. They are found in the rainforests of Malaysia and South America.

Tapirs use their long noses to sniff out fallen fruit and other food.

Rotting leaves

The forest floor is covered in a thin layer of rotting leaves. Because the forest is warm and damp, the leaves rot (break down) very quickly.

Did you know?

A leafcutter ant can carry almost 10 times its own weight. That is like a human lifting a small car above his or her head.

Big cat

The jaguar is a large hunter that eats birds, tapirs and even crocodiles. The dark spots on its coat help it to hide in the shadows on the forest floor.

Leafcutter ants use the pieces of leaf to grow a fungus that the ants eat.

Leafcutters

Leafcutter ants use their jaws to cut out bits of leaves to take back to their nests. Long lines of leafcutter ants can be seen in the forest, stretching from the treetops to the forest floor, where the ants have their nests.

The Tiger

Tigers are the largest of all the cats. They are powerful hunters that eat pigs, deer and young elephants. Sadly, their numbers are falling, because their habitat is being destroyed and people are killing them for their fur and bones.

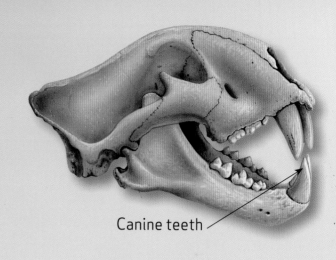

Canine teeth

Sharp teeth

The pointed teeth near the front of the tiger's mouth are about 10 centimetres long. They are called canine teeth. Tigers use their canine teeth to stab and grip prey.

Siberian tigers

Siberian tigers are the largest of all the tigers. They are found in the mountains along the border between Russia and China. Siberian tigers have thicker coats than other tigers because they have to live in very cold conditions.

Nearly half of all the tigers left in the wild are Bengal tigers.

The Bengal tiger

Some Bengal tigers have white fur with pale stripes. Male Bengal tigers are about 3 metres long and weigh up to 220 kilograms, or the weight of three adult humans.

Tiger cubs

A female tiger gives birth to two or three cubs. The cubs stay with their mother for about 18 months while they learn how to hunt.

Tiger facts

🐾 Tigers are found in India, Nepal, China, South-East Asia and eastern Russia.

🐾 In the wild, tigers can live for up to 15 years. In zoos, they will live much longer.

🐾 There are only 3,200 tigers left in the wild.

Warm Grasslands

Grasslands are large areas of flat ground covered by grasses. Warm grasslands, or savannahs, are found in Africa, South America and Australia. During the dry months, the grasses turn yellow. However, once the rains fall, the grasslands turn green.

A sea of grass

Some of the grasses on the savannah are taller than people. There are only a few trees, such as acacias and baobabs. Most of the young trees are eaten before they can grow very tall.

Bone-crushing hyenas

Spotted hyenas are hunters that live on the grasslands of Africa. They have strong jaws and huge teeth that can crush the bones of their prey as if they were twigs.

The great migration

Each year, huge herds of zebras and wildebeest make long journeys in search of fresh grass to eat. This is called a migration. The migration is dangerous, as the animals have to cope with fast-flowing rivers and with hunters, such as crocodiles.

Meerkats keep a keen eye out for hunters, such as snakes, jackals and hawks.

On guard

Meerkats live in large groups in burrows under the grasslands of southern Africa. Each member of the group has a job to do. Some are babysitters or teachers, while others are guards or hunters.

Grazing Animals

The long grasses on the savannah plains attract lots of grass-eating, or grazing, animals. When food and water are scarce, these animals join together in huge herds.

Giraffes

The giraffe has a long neck and long legs. These let it eat the leaves at the tops of trees that other animals cannot reach.

Impalas

Impalas are grazing animals that live in small herds. Green shoots of grass are their favourite food. These shoots appear soon after it rains.

Single toes

Zebras have long legs. These end in a single toe. The toes are protected by hard coverings called hooves.

Hoof

Chewing the cud

Large stomach

Intestines

A grazing animal swallows its food quickly when it eats. The food sits in its stomach before being brought up again into its mouth to chew. This is called chewing the cud and it helps to break up tough grass.

Waterholes

Waterholes are pools of water on the grasslands. These pools are very important, as they are the only sources of drinking water during the dry season, when the rains stop.

Hunters

There are many hunting animals, or predators, living on the savannah. They are attracted by the herds of grazing animals. Predators include lions, leopards, cheetahs and birds of prey.

Running fast

The cheetah is the world's fastest runner. Its thin body and long legs are perfect for running very fast.

Working together

Lions work as a team when they hunt. Some of the lions lie in wait, while others chase an animal towards them. By hunting together, they can catch and pull down large animals such as wildebeest.

Did you know?
Cheetahs can run at speeds of up to 100 kilometres per hour.

Birds of prey
Birds of prey look for prey while they are flying high above the ground. When they spot something to eat, they swoop down on and attack the prey with their claws and beaks.

Cheetahs use their tails for balance when they are running fast.

Hunting in packs
African wild dogs live together in large groups called packs. They hunt as a team and take turns in chasing an animal to tire it out before catching it.

Termites

Termites are small insects that live together in huge groups called colonies. They build enormous nests that stretch far above and below the ground.

The worker termites that build the nests are blind.

Worker termites

Most of the termites in a colony are worker termites. These are the termites that build the nest and find food. They are just a few millimetres long and are a pale cream colour.

Termite facts

- There are more than 2000 different kinds, or species, of termite.
- Worker termites live most of their lives underground and in the nest.
- Termites build their nests from clay, earth or wood, which they mix with saliva (spit) from their mouths.
- Termites can cause lots of damage by chewing the wood of buildings.

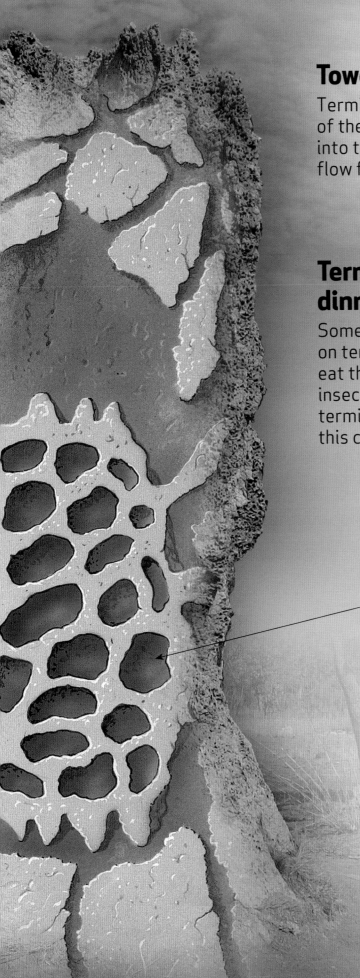

Towering chimneys

Termites live in large pillars called mounds. Some of the largest termite mounds rise several metres into the air. These towers are designed to let air flow freely through them to keep the nest cool.

Termites for dinner

Some animals feed on termites and can eat thousands of the insects in a day. These termite eaters include this carmine bee-eater.

The inside of a termite nest has thousands of tunnels and chambers.

Inside a nest

As well as stretching high above the ground, termites' nests reach deep into the ground. Here, there are underground chambers where the queen termite lays her eggs and where the workers store food.

Scavengers

Animals that feed on the dead remains of other animals are called scavengers. Scavengers on the savannah include vultures, jackals and dung beetles.

Jackals follow lions and will finish off any meat that the lions leave on a dead body.

Stealing food

Some hunters, such as this jackal, are scavengers. They have found that it is easier to eat dead animals or to steal an animal killed by another hunter than to kill prey themselves.

Vultures

Vultures can spot a dead animal on the ground from high in the sky. They glide down to the ground and are soon joined by other vultures to pick over the body.

Did you know?

Sometimes, two or three dung beetles fight over a small ball of dung.

Cleaning up

Dung beetles use their sense of smell to find fresh dung on the ground. They roll the dung into a ball and push it into a hole in the ground beside their eggs. The young beetles feed on the dung when they hatch.

Keeping clean

The heads and necks of vultures are either covered in short feathers or they have no feathers at all. This allows the vultures to stick their heads right inside a dead body and not get any long feathers covered in blood.

Vultures have sharp beaks to rip meat off a dead body.

Deserts

Deserts are places that have very little rain. Some deserts are hot, but there are cold deserts, too. The animals that live in deserts have to be able to survive in a dry place.

Sand dunes

Sand dunes are formed by the wind blowing the sand into piles. Some animals burrow into the dunes to escape the heat and cold.

Did you know?

The largest hot desert in the world is the Sahara in North Africa. It is almost the same size as the United States of America.

The Atacama

The centre of the Atacama Desert in South America is the driest place on the Earth. In some parts, rain has not fallen for hundreds of years. Animals that live here are only found near the coast, where there is water.

North America

The deserts of North America have more plant life than many other deserts. These plants include small bushes and cacti. Some animals make their homes in the cacti or feed on their flowers and fruit.

The cactus stores water inside its stem.

Cold deserts

Antarctica lies around the South Pole. It is the coldest place in the world, but so little rain and snow fall that the region is called a desert. Despite this, lots of animals visit Antarctica to feed and breed during the summer months. These include whales, penguins and seals.

Locust swarms

Locusts form groups called swarms. They fly out of the desert and eat whole crops in neighbouring regions.

Hot Deserts

Most deserts are hot during the day, so animals creep under bushes or into holes to escape the sun. At night, the temperatures fall and it can be very cold.

The bat-eared fox's large ears are very good at hearing prey running across the sand.

Night-time hunter

Bat-eared foxes avoid the heat of the desert by sleeping in burrows during the day. They come out to hunt at night, when it is cooler.

Geckos

Geckos are small lizards. They run on the tips of their feet so that they do not get burned by the hot desert sand.

Geckos lick their eyeballs to stop them from drying out.

Did you know?

Scientists have discovered remains of giant scorpions that were between 70 and 90 centimetres long. These prehistoric monsters lived 330 million years ago.

The sting of some scorpions can kill people.

Scorpions

Some scorpions live in deserts. They are nocturnal, which means that they are active at night. They ambush prey and sting it with their tail stings before eating it.

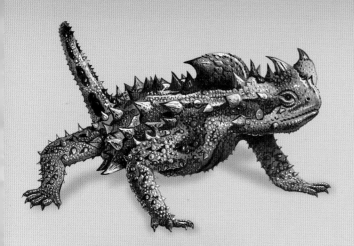

Desert Reptiles

Reptiles are animals that have a scaly skin. They include snakes and lizards. The scaly skin stops their bodies from losing too much water in the dry desert.

Thorny devils

These strange-looking lizards live in the deserts of Australia. Their bodies are covered with very sharp spines. These help to keep hunters away.

Tortoises have a thick shell to protect them from hunters.

The desert tortoise

Desert tortoises get water by eating plants. They store this water in their bodies and use it when they cannot find any plants to eat.

Poisonous rattlesnakes

Rattlesnakes are poisonous snakes that have rattles at the ends of their tails. They shake their rattles when they are threatened, as a warning to other animals. Their sharp teeth inject poison when the snakes bite. This poison kills or paralyses their prey.

Sidewinders

Sidewinders are snakes that can move over hot sand without getting burned. They move sideways, with just a few parts of their bodies touching the sand. The snakes leave behind a series of lines in the sand as their tracks.

Tracks

The Camel

The camel is an expert at surviving in the desert. It can go for two weeks without water. A camel can even drink salty water that would kill other animals.

One hump

Dromedary camels are found in the hot deserts of Africa and the Middle East. They have a single hump on their backs.

Camel facts

- Camels have large, broad feet that are ideal for walking through the desert, as they do not sink into the sand.

- Most people think that a camel's hump is full of water. Instead, it is full of fat. A camel uses this fat when it cannot find enough food to eat.

Bactrian camels have thick coats to keep them warm.

Two humps

Bactrian camels have two humps on their backs. They are found in the cold deserts of China and Central Asia.

Did you know?

Camels have been used to carry goods for humans for more than 4500 years.

A camel's ears are lined with thick hair to keep out sand. ⟶

Desert protection

The camel has long eyelashes to protect its eyes from the sun and blowing sand. Its nostrils can close tightly shut to keep out any sand.

Cool Grasslands

Grasslands found in the cooler parts of the world are called temperate grasslands. These regions are warm in the summer and they may be covered in snow in the winter.

Did you know?

Some kinds of porcupine have 30,000 or more pointed quills on their backs.

What's in a name?

Temperate grasslands are called different names in different parts of the world. In North America they are called prairies. In South America they are called pampas and in Asia they are known as steppes.

Herd animals

Some plant-eating animals join together in huge herds, or groups, on the grasslands. These include the pronghorn, which is a kind of antelope that lives in North America.

Sharp points

Porcupines are covered in thousands of sharp spines called quills. When attacked, they turn their backs on their enemy and raise their quills to protect themselves.

Porcupine quills break off easily and remain stuck in an attacker.

Prairie hunters

There are a number of predators, or hunters, on the prairie, such as coyotes. They hunt hares and small deer, on their own or in packs. Coyotes communicate by making long, loud howls.

Grassland Mammals

Lots of plant-eating mammals are attracted to grasslands because there is plenty of food. These plant eaters also attract hunters that come looking for animals to eat.

Digging hunter

The badger uses its long, sharp claws to dig small animals, such as ground squirrels and mice, out of the ground.

Rabbits thump the ground with their back legs to warn other rabbits of danger.

Good listener

The rabbit has long ears, which give it a good sense of hearing. It uses these to listen for any hunters that may be nearby.

Red fox

The red fox is a carnivore, or meat eater. It is usually active at night, when it hunts for small mammals, such as rabbits. It also feeds on berries.

Did you know?

A single pair of rabbits will have as many as 40 babies in a year.

Pack animals

Llamas are found on the grassy slopes of the Andes Mountains in South America. These plant eaters live in groups called herds and are used by local people to carry heavy loads.

Llamas are related to camels.

American Bison

The American bison is the largest land mammal in North America. It is easily recognized by its extra large head and shoulders and its shaggy coat.

Bison facts

- When attacked by wolves or other large hunters, bison form a circle around their young with their horns pointing outwards.
- Adult bison can weigh up to 900 kilograms. That is as much as 12 adult humans.
- The bison is also called the American buffalo.

Keeping sharp

Both the male and female bison have a pair of short, curved horns. They rub their horns against trees or rocks to keep them sharp.

Bison use their horns to fight each other.

Did you know?

Bison can run very quickly. They can reach speeds of 73 kilometres per hour.

Return of the bison

During the late 1800s, human hunters killed nearly all of the bison. Only 1000 or so survived. Today, they are protected by law and their numbers are increasing.

Surviving the cold

At the start of winter, bison move from the grasslands to valleys and wooded areas, where they can shelter from the cold winter storms.

Living under the Grassland

A large number of animals live under grasslands. Many dig deep holes, called burrows, in the soil. Others use the holes for shelter.

Prairie dogs

Prairie dogs are named after their call, which sounds like a dog's bark. They live together in large groups and dig a maze of burrows, which is called a town.

Did you know?

One hundred years ago, there were as many as 5 billion prairie dogs living on the grasslands of North America.

Tunnelling moles

Moles are small animals with large front feet that are shaped like spades. They use their feet to dig tunnels through the soil. Moles feed on worms and other small animals that fall into the tunnels.

Prairie dogs

Burrowing owl

Badger

Rabbit

Ferret

Salamander

Living in tunnels

Tunnels dug by prairie dogs and moles can be homes to other animals. These include salamanders, which are related to frogs and toads. There is even a kind of bird, called the burrowing owl, which lives in tunnels underground. Hunters, such as snakes, ferrets and badgers, also move into the burrows.

Wombats

Wombats are night-time plant eaters that are found only in Australia. They live in burrows that can be up to 20 metres long and lie more than two metres below the ground.

Living in the Trees

Many kinds of animal make their homes in trees all around the world. Trees give them both food and shelter.

Fussy eater

Koalas live in the forests of Australia and they eat only leaves from eucalyptus trees. Koalas sleep during the day, when it is hot, and become active at sunset.

Koalas rarely drink water. They usually get the liquid they need from leaves.

Building a nest

Many birds make their nests from materials they find in the forests. They collect twigs, leaves, moss, feathers and bits of sheep's fleece to use in their nests.

Tree frogs

Most frogs live on the ground, but tree frogs live high up in rainforest trees. They have sticky pads at the tips of their toes that help them to grip branches.

Squirrels use their bushy tails to keep warm at night.

Did you know?

Eucalyptus leaves are poisonous to most animals. But koalas can destroy the poisons inside their bodies, making the leaves safe to eat.

The red squirrel

The red squirrel has reddish brown fur and long ear tufts. It is found in northern forests and feeds on seeds and nuts.

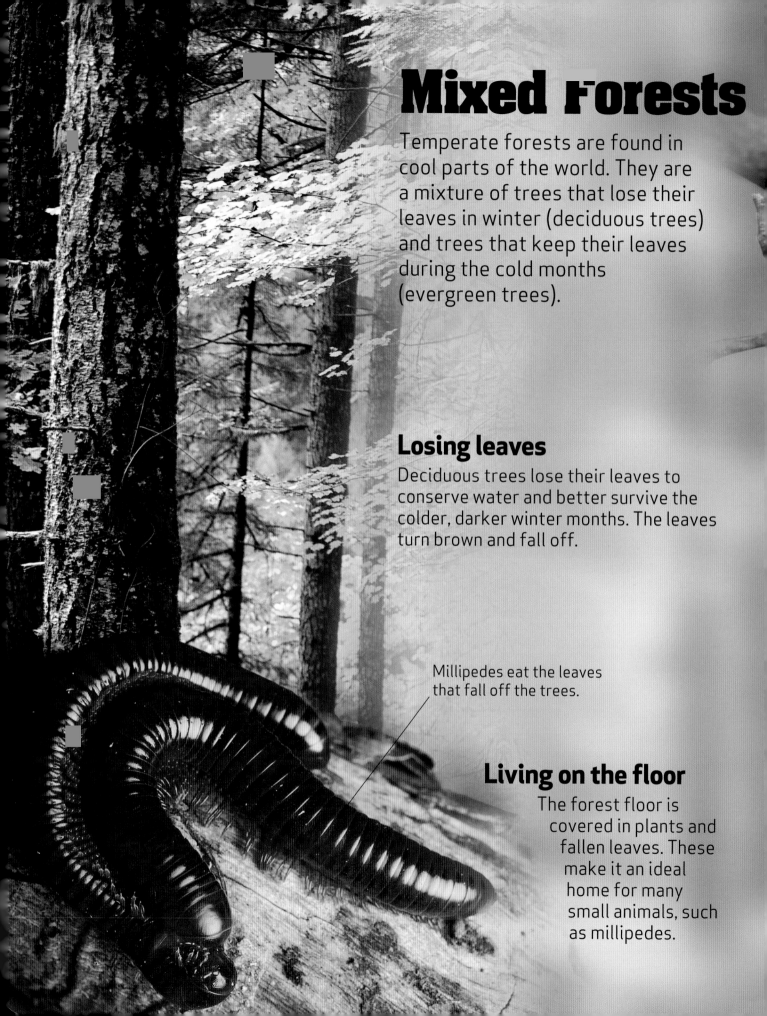

Mixed Forests

Temperate forests are found in cool parts of the world. They are a mixture of trees that lose their leaves in winter (deciduous trees) and trees that keep their leaves during the cold months (evergreen trees).

Losing leaves

Deciduous trees lose their leaves to conserve water and better survive the colder, darker winter months. The leaves turn brown and fall off.

Millipedes eat the leaves that fall off the trees.

Living on the floor

The forest floor is covered in plants and fallen leaves. These make it an ideal home for many small animals, such as millipedes.

Forest birds

Temperate forests are home to many birds. The birds eat the seeds and fruit that grow on the trees, as well as insects living there. The birds also build nests in the branches.

Wrens hunt for insects in holes and cracks on trees.

Wild boar

Wild boar are large pigs that live in forests. They eat roots, fruit and berries that lie on the forest floor. Male boars have curved teeth, called tusks, which stick out of their mouths.

Did you know?

The largest tree, the sequoia, can grow to more than 100 metres tall and live for 2000 years.

Woodland Insects

Many insects lay their eggs on trees. When the eggs hatch, the young insects are then near to their favourite food – leaves.

This caterpillar is brightly coloured as a warning that it is poisonous.

Caterpillars

Caterpillars are the larvae, or young, of butterflies and moths. They eat leaves and grow in size before they turn into adult moths and butterflies.

Some caterpillars look like small twigs.

Clever hiders

Many caterpillars are difficult to see on trees. Some are coloured green so that they blend in with the leaves. This makes them hard for hunters to spot.

Insect hunters

The insects living among the leaves attract many woodland birds, such as blue tits. These birds pick the insects out of the bark on the trees. They eat the insects or feed them to their young.

Blue tits build their nests inside holes in tree trunks.

All about galls

Galls are small balls that grow on leaves and branches. The galls are made by insects called gall wasps. The wasps lay their eggs inside a leaf, branch or bud. As the egg hatches and the young wasp grows, the plant swells to form a gall with the insect inside.

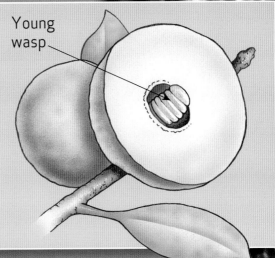

Young wasp

Woodland Floor

The woodland floor is damp and shady, and is covered in a thick layer of leaves and twigs. Many animals live here, hiding from hunters and looking for something to eat.

Stag beetles

Young stag beetles, or larvae, grow up on the forest floor. The adult males have huge jaws, which they use to fight each other.

Did you know?

When two male stag beetles fight, the winner is the beetle that can flip its opponent over.

Woodland mice

During the day, woodland mice hide in small tunnels to avoid hunters. At night, they come out and look for seeds, fruit, nuts and small insects to eat.

Wolf spiders bite
their prey with
their huge fangs.

Wolf spiders

Unlike many other spiders, wolf spiders do not make
webs. Instead, they chase their prey on the ground.
When they catch an animal, they inject it with poison
so that it stops moving.

Woodcocks use their long
bills to pick earthworms
out from the soil.

Ground nesting

The woodcock nests on
the woodland floor. The
female bird has patchy
coloured feathers that
blend with the dead
leaves on the ground.
This hides her when she
is on the nest.

Surviving Winter

Winter is a difficult time for animals. There is little food to eat and water can be frozen solid. Animals find different ways of surviving the cold winter months.

Storing squirrels

During the autumn, squirrels bury food, such as nuts, in the ground. In the winter, they dig the nuts up again to eat.

Woodland deer

Deer shelter in woodlands throughout the winter, nibbling buds off the ends of branches. They also push snow to one side with their feet so that they can find food.

Sleeping skunks

Striped skunks go to sleep for several days at a time during the winter. On milder winter days, they wake up and hunt for food.

Skunks protect themselves by spraying a smelly liquid at attackers.

Hibernation

Some animals, such as dormice, survive the winter by crawling into a safe place and going into a very deep sleep. This is called hibernation. The animals wake up when the weather gets warmer in spring.

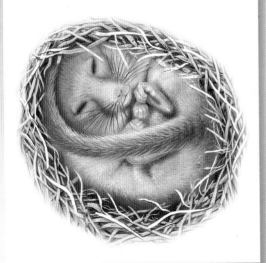

Migrating birds

Birds such as swallows avoid the cold weather by flying to warmer parts of the world. Once the winter has finished and the weather gets warmer, the birds fly back. This journey is called a migration.

Northern Forests

A band of evergreen forest stretches across the top of North America, Europe and Asia. The trees that grow here are called conifers. Winters are long and cold, and there are fewer animals than in warmer forests because there is little food to eat.

Grazing deer

Large deer live in the northern coniferous forests, feeding off grass, twigs and bark. Some deer grow enormous antlers on top of their heads. At the end of each year, these antlers drop off and new ones start to grow.

Male white-tailed deer use their antlers to fight each other in autumn. This is called rutting.

Sharp leaves

Conifer trees have leaves shaped like needles. These leaves are adapted to cold conditions and designed to be tough to reduce water loss.

Laying eggs

The wood wasp, or horntail, lays its eggs in the bark of conifer trees. The female has a long, pointed tube at the end of her body, which she digs into the bark to lay her eggs.

Egg-laying tube

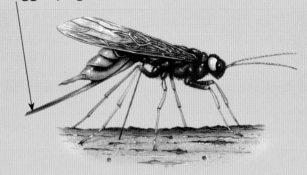

Team birds

The northern forests are home to many birds. This blue jay lives in forests in North America. Blue jays will work together and attack other animals that get too near their nests.

Forest hunters

The lynx is one of the hunting animals that live in the northern forests. It climbs up a tree and waits for an animal to pass close by before leaping down and attacking.

The Brown Bear

Brown bears are found in Europe, Asia and North America. They live in forests, on grasslands and on mountains. They have thick, furry coats that are grey, brown or even black in colour.

Brown bear facts

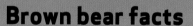 Bears can run at speeds of up to 55 kilometres per hour.

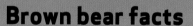 Brown bears are omnivorous. This means that they will eat any kind of food, including meat and plants.

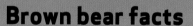 Male brown bears are much larger than female bears. In some cases, the male can be twice as large as the female.

Large animals

The largest brown bears are found on Kodiak Island in Alaska, United States. They can weigh more than 600 kilograms – that is as much as eight adult humans!

Catching salmon

In autumn, brown bears feast on salmon. They stand in rivers and catch the fish with their jaws and long claws.

Some bears stand on top of waterfalls and catch salmon as they jump up.

A mouthful of teeth

Bears use their teeth to catch prey, and also to attack other bears. They have a pair of long, sharp teeth at the front of their mouths for gripping animals.

Looking for food

Bears will eat anything! They will even raid human campsites and rubbish bins looking for something to eat.

Birds of the Forest

Mixed forests are home to lots of different birds. These birds shelter and nest in the trees. Some only visit the forests in the winter, but others stay all year round.

Woodpeckers

Woodpeckers make their nests in holes tree trunks. They hammer their strong beaks against the trunks to dig out the holes.

Did you know?

Woodpeckers have four toes on their feet. Two point forwards and two point backwards. This helps them to climb up and down a tree trunk easily.

Ghost of the forest

The great grey owl has grey feathers with black and white spots. These make the owl look like it is a ghost.

Wild turkeys

Wild turkeys live in forests
in North America. They
spend most of their time on
the ground, but they can fly
up to 500 metres to escape
an attacker.

Turkeys have
small, weak wings,
so they can fly only
short distances.

Goshawks eat
rabbits and
squirrels.

Goshawks

The goshawk is a bird of
prey – that is, a bird that
hunts other animals.
Goshawks have very good
eyesight and can spot
their prey from high up
in the sky.

Frozen Wastes

North of the coniferous forests lies an icy wasteland called the tundra. This region is frozen throughout the winter, but bursts into life when the snow melts in the short summer months.

Fierce wolverines

The wolverine looks like a small bear, but it is related to the weasel. It lives in the northern forests and the tundra and has a thick coat of fur to protect it from the cold.

Always frozen

Just beneath the surface of the tundra, the soil is always frozen. This stops plants with large roots, such as trees, from growing there. But during the summer, small plants, such as this Arctic poppy, burst into bloom.

Tundra plains

When the summer arrives, the snow melts and forms pools on the tundra's surface. The soil becomes soft enough for small animals to burrow into, seeking shelter or food.

Snow geese

Snow geese fly to the
tundra in the summer
to raise their young.
In autumn, they fly
south to warmer areas.

Snow geese fly
in large flocks,
or groups.

Herds of reindeer

Reindeer move into the tundra
in the summer to give birth to their
young. When winter comes, the
reindeer herds return to the
coniferous forests.

Did you know?

The Arctic tundra
covers one tenth of
the Earth's total
surface.

The Arctic

The Arctic is the region around the North Pole. This icy world has very long winters. In the middle of winter, the sun sets and does not rise again for several weeks.

Changing ice sheet

The Arctic is covered by a thick sheet of ice. During the summer, some of the ice melts and the sheet gets smaller. This means that land hunters, such as polar bears, have less area to hunt in, and they can struggle to find food.

Keeping warm

Seals have a thick layer of fat, called blubber, just beneath their skin. This keeps the seals warm in the icy Arctic seas.

Multicoloured beaks

Puffins catch small fish to eat and to feed to their young. They hold the fish in their colourful beaks and can carry about 10 fish at a time.

Did you know?

Puffins are very good swimmers and can dive to depths of 60 metres to look for fish.

A new coat

The Arctic fox changes the colour of its coat during the year to blend in with its surroundings. In winter, it has a white coat to hide in the snow. In summer, it turns brown to match the rocks and soil.

Travelling Animals

During the summer, many animals travel to the Arctic to feed and breed. When it gets colder in the autumn, they move away again. This journey is called migration.

Huge herds of caribou travel hundreds of kilometres to the tundra and back.

Migrating caribou

Caribou are reindeer that live in North America. They spend the winter in the forests, but move north in summer to give birth to their calves and to feed on the Arctic tundra.

Hunting wolves

Wolves follow the caribou on their migration, hunting the older and weaker animals. They are very good runners and will follow herds of caribou for up to 20 kilometres every day.

Did you know?

An Arctic tern can live for 20 years. This means that one tern may fly around the world 20 times during its lifetime.

Record traveller

Arctic terns make the longest migration of any animal. They breed in the Arctic in summer and fly to Antarctica for winter, before returning to the Arctic. That is a round trip of at least 32,000 kilometres.

ARCTIC

Arctic tern migration routes

Arctic terns follow the coasts of Europe, Africa or the Americas on their long migration.

ANTARCTICA

The Polar Bear

Polar bears are the world's largest land hunters. They usually live on their own, prowling over the Arctic ice looking for seals to eat.

Polar bears have even caught beluga whales to eat.

Fur coat

Polar bears have thick coats of transparent fur that reflects the white of the snow, so that they blend in and cannot be seen by their prey. Beneath the fur is a thick layer of fat. The fur and fat help to keep the polar bear warm.

Too hot!

The fur and fat on polar bears are so good at trapping heat that the animals can get too warm in the summer. They have to lie down on the ice to cool off.

Bear watching

Watching polar bears is very popular in Canada. People use special vehicles so that they can get close to the animals.

Polar bear facts

🐾 The soles of a polar bear's feet are very rough. This stops the bear from slipping around on the ice.

🐾 Adult male polar bears can weigh up to 680 kilograms – that is about the weight of nine adult humans.

🐾 When it is very cold, some polar bears cover their faces to stop their bodies losing heat through their noses.

Strong swimmers

Polar bears are excellent swimmers. They use their large feet to paddle through the icy water. Some bears have been seen swimming 100 kilometres from land.

Antarctica

Antarctica is the region around the South Pole. Unlike the Arctic, there is a large amount of land in Antarctica, which is covered by thick ice. These cold conditions make life very harsh for the animals living here.

Food for all

Many animals visit Antarctica in the summer. Tiny plants and animals in the sea, called plankton, increase in number as the weather gets warmer. The plankton attract fish, which provide food for seals and penguins.

Leopard seals

Leopard seals are fierce hunters. As well as eating fish and squid, they also eat penguins and other seals.

Polar tourists

Very few people live in Antarctica, but more and more people are visiting the region as tourists. These tourists need to be very careful that they do not damage the area by dropping litter or disturbing the animals.

Swimming birds

Many penguins lay their eggs and raise their young in Antarctica. They warm their eggs in folds of skin by their feet.

Chinstrap penguins are named after the thin band of black feathers that runs under their chins.

Penguins

Penguins are swimming birds that live in the Earth's southern hemisphere (the southern half of our planet). They have webbed feet and flipper-like wings, which they use to swim.

Keeping warm

Unlike other birds, penguins have feathers all the way down their legs. They also have a thick layer of fat under their skin. These help to keep them warm in the cold Antarctic.

Emperor penguins take good care of their young.

Penguin facts

🐾 Emperor penguins are the largest penguins. They can weigh nearly 45 kilograms – that is the weight of 45 large bags of flour!

🐾 The largest penguin colonies contain more than 10 million birds.

Huge colonies

When it is time to breed, penguins gather together in large groups called colonies. They huddle together to keep each other warm.

The jackass penguin

Jackass penguins get their name from the loud braying noise that they make, which sounds like a donkey. They are found on the beaches of southern Africa.

Flying underwater

Penguins are clumsy on land but are graceful and fast in water. The surface of their bodies is smooth so that they slip through the water easily. They find it difficult to walk on land and often slide along the snow on their bellies.

Jackass penguins are about 70 centimetres tall and weigh up to 4 kilograms.

Farmland

Large areas of land have been cleared around the world to make space for farms. Wild animals come to this farmland to eat the crops or to hunt smaller animals.

Farming fields

Farmland has a mixture of habitats. There may be hedgerows between fields and small pockets of woodland. There are also meadows, which are fields where farm animals graze. These may be full of wild flowers.

Butterfly meadows

Meadows are important habitats for insects. In early summer, the grasses are tall and there are lots of flowers, which attract butterflies and bees.

This red admiral butterfly feeds on nectar, a sugary liquid in flowers.

Farm animals

People have been farming animals, such as cows, sheep and pigs, for thousands of years. We farm these animals because we can use the milk, meat and wool that they produce.

Bumblebees

Bumblebees visit the flowers that grow in meadows and hedgerows. They collect nectar and carry it back to their hives, or nests. They use the nectar to feed themselves.

Did you know?

Bees fly up to 14 kilometres from their hives in search of flowers.

Seed eaters

Farmland is good for birds because it provides plenty of food. Seed-eating birds, such as goldfinches, have short, strong beaks that are ideal for cracking open seeds.

Living in Cities

Many animals live close to people – in parks and gardens, in homes and under the ground in sewers. These animals include foxes, squirrels, rats and pigeons.

City homes

Cities make ideal homes for some animals. There are lots of places to shelter or build nests. There is plenty of food, too. This can be found in rubbish bags, in litter on the streets and in homes.

Foxes are related to dogs and wolves.

Urban foxes

The red fox has become used to living close to people. It visits gardens and parks at night, and finds food in rubbish bins.

Racoons

Racoons are found in North America, where they often visit gardens and parks. These clever animals use their long fingers to open bags and boxes to get at any food inside.

Falcons eat other birds and small mammals, such as mice.

City pigeons

Pigeons are a common sight in many cities. They gather together in parks and other open spaces looking for food. They can be a nuisance, as their droppings make a lot of mess.

Nesting falcons

Peregrine falcons build their nests on high buildings. From here, they have a good view of any prey moving around below.

Living in Caves

Many caves are cold and damp and often lie far below ground. Very little light can reach these places, and the animals that live there have to cope with complete darkness.

Bat caves

Bats sleep, or roost, in caves during the day, hanging upside down with their claws gripping the cave walls. At night, they fly out of the cave to hunt for food.

Caves

Caves range in size from small hollows in a cliff to enormous cave networks that are hundreds of kilometres long.

No eyes

The blind cave fish has no eyes. This is not a problem because the caves are dark, so the fish does not need to see. Instead, it relies on its other senses to move around and find food.

Cave spiders

Cave spiders are very common in many parts of the world. They lay their eggs in large sacs shaped like teardrops, which hang from the cave roof.

Did you know?

The tiny tooth cave spider is just 1.6 millimetres long. This minute hunter spins webs on cave walls in Texas, United States.

Cave spiders hunt small insects and woodlice.

Mountains

Mountains have many different kinds of habitat. There are thick rainforests and meadows, as well as steep slopes covered in rocks and fast-flowing streams.

Eagle's nest

Golden eagles build huge nests, or eyries, on cliffs and mountains. They are strong hunters, catching mice, hares and even deer.

Golden eagles glide on wings that can measure 2.5 metres across.

Changing habitats

Habitats on a mountain change with the altitude, or height. At the bottom, there are forests. Higher up, the trees stop and are replaced by grasslands. At the very top, there are a few small plants and little else.

Mountain gorilla

Mountain gorillas are found in rainforests on the mountains of central Africa. They have thick coats that help them stay warm during the cold mountain nights.

Did you know?

Snow leopards wrap their long, thick tails around their faces to keep their noses and lungs warm at night.

Mountain hunters

Snow leopards are found in the mountains of Asia. They are strong hunters that usually hunt sheep and goats. Once snow leopards have killed their prey, they stay close to the body to stop other animals from stealing it.

Snow leopards are strong enough to kill prey three times their size.

Life on Rocks and Snow

Few animals can survive at the tops of mountains. There is very little to eat, and the ground is covered in large, slippery boulders. Temperatures are low and snow lies on the ground all year round.

Did you know?

Mountain goats can leap 3 metres from one ledge to another. They can also turn around on ledges that are only a few centimetres wide.

Mountain movers

Bighorn sheep move up mountains during the summer to feed on grasses on the high slopes. When winter comes, they move down again to escape the snow.

Bighorn sheep like open ground, where they can easily spot any attackers.

Yaks

The yak is a large, shaggy animal that lives in the Himalaya Mountains in Asia. It has a thick coat to keep it warm in the cold mountain air.

Sure-footed goats

Mountain goats are found on the steepest cliffs, where they leap from ledge to ledge. They can do this because they have special hooves that grip the rock.

The name marmot comes from an old French word meaning 'mountain mouse'.

Whistling warning

Marmots are small animals that live in large groups on mountain slopes. Their warning call is a high-pitched whistle. When other marmots hear this whistle, they know danger is near and run into their burrows.

LIVING IN THE AIR

Many animals have learned how to fly through the air. These include birds, insects and bats. They fly using wings made from feathers or flaps of skin, which they flap to lift them off the ground. Flying lets these animals hunt for food in the air and helps them to escape from predators.

Birds

Birds are animals that are covered in feathers. These keep them warm and help them fly. Birds also have wings instead of arms, and a hard bill, or beak, which they use to collect food.

Hunting birds

Birds that hunt other animals are called birds of prey. They have large, hooked beaks and huge claws, called talons, which they use to collect food.

Buzzards fly high in the air, keeping an eye out for prey.

Kingfishers use their long bills to catch fish.

Colourful feathers

Some birds, such as kingfishers, have very bright and colourful feathers. This is usually to attract a partner. Birds will sometimes perform a special dance to make themselves look even more attractive.

Waterproof feathers

Birds that live in water, such as ducks, have oily feathers. This stops water from soaking into their feathers. Otherwise, the birds would sink.

Mallards are sometimes called dabbling ducks. They dabble, or dip, for pondweed.

Did you know?

The peregrine falcon is the fastest animal in the world. When it dives down to catch its prey, it can reach speeds of up to 270 kilometres per hour.

Preening

Birds look after their feathers by keeping them clean. This is called preening. They use their beaks to straighten any bent feathers.

Birds' Wings

Birds have wings instead of arms. They fly by extending and flapping their wings. The wings are made from a number of bones with feathers attached to them. They can be long and broad or short and narrow.

Some gannets have wings that measure nearly two metres across.

Gliding through air

Gliding birds, such as gannets, use currents of moving air to fly. These birds have very large wings that catch the currents and carry the birds into the air.

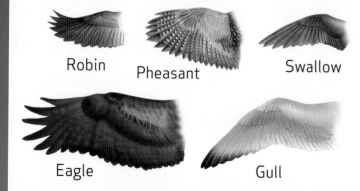

Robin

Pheasant

Swallow

Eagle

Gull

Wing shapes

Birds that fly by gliding and soaring, such as eagles and gulls, have large, narrow wings with long feathers. Birds that fly short distances and need to dart about quickly, such as robins, pheasants and swallows, have short wings, which they flap quickly.

Silent fliers

Some owls do not make a sound when they fly. They have soft feathers along the fronts of their wings, which quieten the sound of the air as it passes over the wings.

Fast flight

Swallows have short wings that let them fly quickly and dart about to catch flying insects. If they need to dive, they pull their wings into their bodies and drop like a stone.

Some hummingbirds flap their wings 1200 times a minute.

Hovering hummingbirds

Hummingbirds are small birds that can hover. They stay in one place by beating their wings backwards and forwards very quickly. This allows them to hover in front of a flower so that they can reach in and drink nectar.

The Bald Eagle

Bald eagles are birds of prey. This means that they eat other animals. They have very good eyesight, which they use to spot their prey far below.

Large wingspan

Bald eagles have a wingspan of 2.5 metres. They use their large wings to catch rising currents of warm air and soar high into the sky.

Eagle food

Bald eagles eat small birds, fish and mammals. They will also eat dead animals, especially in winter, when living food is hard to find.

A bald eagle catches a fish with its sharp claws. These claws are called talons.

Did you know?

The name 'bald eagle' does not mean that the bird has no feathers on its head. Instead, the word 'bald' in Old English meant 'white'.

Eagle facts

- An adult female bald eagle weighs just under six kilograms, while the male weighs just over four kilograms.

- Bald eagles live for about 25 years in the wild, but up to 50 years in captivity.

- Young bald eagles are completely brown. The white head feathers do not appear until the bird is four years old.

Nesting eagles

Bald eagles build huge nests called eyries. A pair of eagles always uses the same nest, making it bigger each year. An eagle's nest can weigh more than 450 kilograms, or the weight of six adult humans.

Hooked beaks

Bald eagles have a large, hooked beak. They use this to rip their prey to pieces and tear off chunks of meat to swallow.

Flightless Birds

Flightless birds have feathers and wings but cannot fly. They include the largest birds in the world, such as ostriches, rheas and emus.

Ostriches live on the hot grasslands of Africa.

Fast runners

Ostriches have long, powerful legs, which they use to run away from hunters. They can reach speeds of 65 kilometres per hour.

Cormorants

The flightless cormorant is a bird that lives on the Galapagos Islands. It swims through the sea around the coast, catching fish, squid and octopus to eat.

Kiwis are about the same size as a chicken.

A cassowary has a large bony growth called a casque.

Kiwis of New Zealand

Kiwis live in the forests, swamps and grasslands of New Zealand. They are named after their unusual call, which is a high-pitched whistle. Kiwis have nostrils right at the ends of their long beaks, which they use to sniff out insects.

Cassowary

Cassowaries live in the rainforests of Australia. These tall birds have a razor-sharp claw on the end of each leg, which they use to defend themselves.

Building Nests

Most birds build nests in which they lay their eggs. Different birds build different shapes of nest, which range from simple cup shapes to enormous platforms.

Building materials

Nests are made from a range of materials, such as twigs, leaves, moss, wool and feathers. Some birds even use human rubbish to build their nests.

This paradise flycatcher has made its nest from twigs, leaves and moss.

Swallow nests

Swallows build their nests out of small balls of mud and clay. Each nest can contain 1500 balls of clay.

Did you know?

The vervain hummingbird builds the smallest bird's nest, which is about the size of half a walnut shell.

Weaving a nest

Weaver birds build their nests by weaving thin twigs and reeds together. Woven nests usually have narrow entrances to stop egg-eating animals from getting inside.

Massive platforms

Some birds, such as storks and eagles, build large platform nests out of sticks and twigs. The largest platforms can measure more than two metres across and six metres deep.

A spectacled weaver bird stands at the narrow entrance to its nest.

Small birds, such as blue tits, are safe from hunters in a nest box.

Nest boxes

A good way to attract birds into the garden is to put up a nest box. Birds then build their nest inside the box.

Growing Birds

All birds lay eggs. The parent birds look after the eggs to make sure the chicks, or baby birds, hatch. Then they feed the baby birds until the chicks are big enough to leave the nest.

Keeping warm

Birds' eggs must be kept warm if the chicks are to hatch. The parents do this by sitting on top of the eggs. This is called incubation.

Nest impostors

Cuckoos do not build nests. Instead, they lay their eggs in the nests of other birds, who then look after the baby cuckoos. Baby cuckoos are bigger than the other chicks in the nest, so they get the food.

Baby birds

Newly hatched chicks are weak and parents must give them all the food they need. Sometimes, parents will swallow the food and then bring it back up for the chicks to eat.

Did you know?

Ostriches lay the largest birds' eggs. Each egg is about 18 centimetres long and weighs 1.2 kilograms.

Leaving the nest

As the chicks grow, the parents bring back more and more food. When the chicks are strong enough, they will try a few short practice flights. Then they will leave the nest for good.

This eagle chick is now ready to leave its nest.

Bats

Bats are the only mammals that can fly by flapping rather than gliding. Instead of front legs, they have wings. They do not walk with their back legs, but use them to hang upside down.

Roosting bats

Most bats are nocturnal, which means that they are active at night. They sleep during the day, hanging by their feet from the walls of caves, buildings and trees. This is called roosting.

Did you know?

Some fruit bats have a wingspan of almost two metres. They can use their large wings to keep warm when roosting.

There are nearly 1000 species of bat.

Fruit bats

Fruit bats live in the forests of Africa, Australia and Asia. Some fruit bats have extra-long tongues, which they use to suck nectar out of flowers.

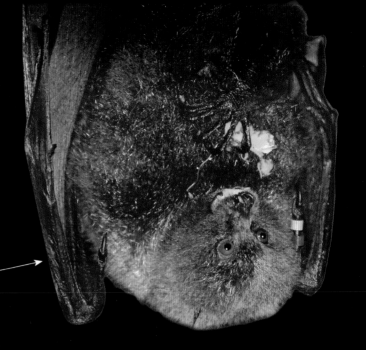

Fruit bats are sometimes called flying foxes.

Bats in flight

A bat has powerful chest muscles, which it uses to flap its wings. It steers by moving the bones in its fingers and legs to change the wings' shape.

The bat wing

The bones in a bat's fingers are extra long and are covered by a thin layer of skin, which forms the wing. A thumb sticks out from the top of the wing and ends in a claw.

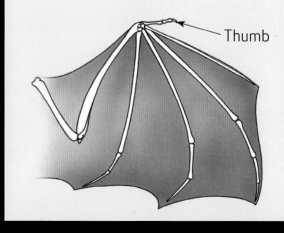

Thumb

Fruit bat camp

Fruit bats gather in large groups high in the branches of rainforest trees. These groups are called camps.

Bat Senses

Most bats hunt at night, when it is too dark to see. Instead of using their eyes, some bats use sounds to detect objects. This is called echolocation.

Large ears

Most bats have large ears, which give them excellent hearing. They use their ears to collect sounds in the dark and to help them locate their prey.

Vampire bats cut the skin of their prey and lap up the blood.

Heat-seeking vampires

Vampires are blood-sucking bats. They feed on the blood of cows, pigs, horses and birds. They detect their prey at night using special heat sensors in their faces.

Hearing in the dark

Echolocation is the use of sounds and echoes to find objects. Bats make very high-pitched sounds. These sounds hit an object and an echo comes back. A bat can tell where this object is, and how big it is, by listening to the echo.

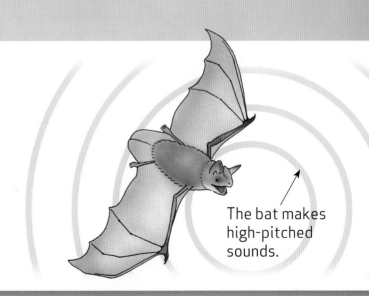

The bat makes high-pitched sounds.

Did you know?

Vampire bats can drink about one and a half times their body weight in blood in one feed. They need to eat at least two tablespoons of blood each day.

Fruit bats have larger eyes than other bats, because they are active during the day.

Large eyes

Fruit bats do not use echolocation. Instead, they have large eyes, which they use to spot fruit in the rainforest. They also use their noses to smell their food.

The sounds bounce off the moth as echoes, and travel back to the bat.

Flying Insects

Most insects have two pairs
of wings, which they use to
fly. Insect wings vary in shape,
from the thin wings of bees
to the large, colourful
wings of butterflies.

Hard to catch

Houseflies have only one pair of
wings, but they are still among the
fastest insects. They use their
speed to escape attackers.

Insect hunters

Dragonflies have two pairs of long,
see-through wings. These powerful
insects are excellent fliers, and
can catch smaller insects
in mid-air.

Dragonflies have large
eyes for spotting prey.

Buzzing bees

The honeybee has two pairs of very thin wings. It beats these wings so quickly that they make a buzzing sound. A bee can fly at 32 kilometres per hour.

Did you know?

Most insects do not use their mouths to make sounds. Instead, they rub their wings or legs together to make a noise.

Colourful butterflies

Butterfly wings are covered in tiny scales. These scales can be a wide range of colours.

Ladybird wings

The ladybird has a pair of tough red and black wings. These cover a second pair of wings, which are very delicate. The ladybird uses the second pair for flying.

Changing Insects

Insects change a lot as they hatch from eggs and grow into adults. Some even change the entire shape of their bodies from long, thin caterpillars into winged moths and butterflies.

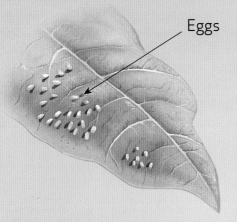

Eggs

Egg

A female butterfly lays tiny eggs on the leaves of plants.

Leaf muncher

The eggs hatch into young insects, called larvae. The larvae of butterflies are known as caterpillars. Caterpillars eat leaves and grow very quickly.

Caterpillar

Butterfly

When the caterpillar has completely changed, the chrysalis splits open and a fully grown butterfly emerges. It spreads its wings so that they can dry. Then it flies away to feed and, if it is a female, to lay more eggs.

Adult butterfly

As a pupa, the caterpillar surrounds itself with a hard case, called a chrysalis.

Hard case

When a caterpillar has reached full size, it turns into a pupa. This is the stage when the insect changes from a caterpillar into a butterfly. This change can take several weeks.

The Desert Locust

Desert locusts are a kind of grasshopper. Unlike most grasshoppers, desert locusts can cause huge amounts of damage by eating all the plants in a region.

A locust's head

A locust has a pair of eyes, plus two feelers on top of its head, called antennae. Its jaws have jagged edges to chew through leaves.

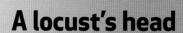

Swarms of locusts can fly up to 130 kilometres in a day.

Huge swarms

Sometimes, locusts join together in massive groups, called swarms. Some swarms are 40 kilometres long and contain billions of insects.

Flying and jumping

An adult locust has two pairs of wings. The front pair is hard and covers the rear pair of wings. Locusts also have a long pair of back legs that they use for jumping.

An adult locust can eat its own weight in food every day.

Locust facts

🐾 Locusts make a chirruping noise by rubbing their long back legs together.

🐾 A large swarm of locusts can eat up to 80,000 tonnes of food in a single day – that's the same weight as 10,000 African elephants.

Rear wings

Hidden wings

The hind, or rear, pair of wings on a locust is only seen when the insect is flying. With these wings, a locust can fly at 20 kilometres per hour.

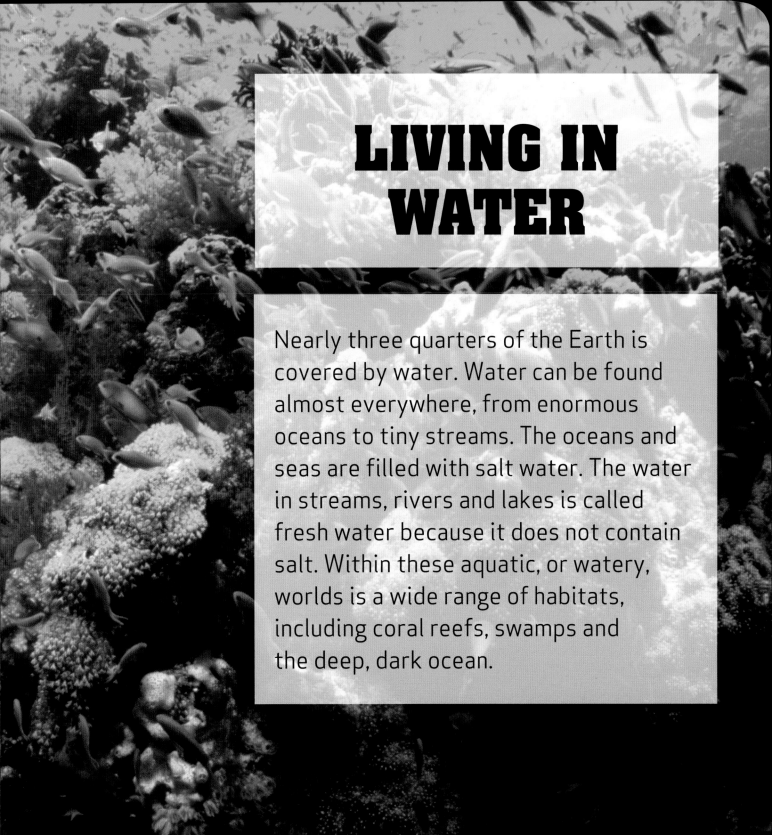

LIVING IN WATER

Nearly three quarters of the Earth is covered by water. Water can be found almost everywhere, from enormous oceans to tiny streams. The oceans and seas are filled with salt water. The water in streams, rivers and lakes is called fresh water because it does not contain salt. Within these aquatic, or watery, worlds is a wide range of habitats, including coral reefs, swamps and the deep, dark ocean.

How do Fish Swim?

Fish have powerful tails, which they move from side to side to push them through the water. They also have a number of fins on their bodies that they use to guide them.

Did you know?
The sailfish is the fastest fish. It can swim at speeds of up to 110 kilometres per hour. This is faster than the fastest land mammal, the cheetah, can run.

Fast-swimming fish

The fastest fish in the seas are sailfish and tuna. Their bodies are streamlined, which means that they are thin and can slip through the water easily.

Tuna

Angelfish

Angelfish have a different body shape from tuna. Their bodies are squashed from side to side. This means that they are not very fast swimmers, but they can twist and turn quickly.

Fish fins

A fish has a number of fins, each with a special job. The pectoral fins and the pelvic fins help with steering and stopping. The dorsal fin helps to keep the fish upright in the water.

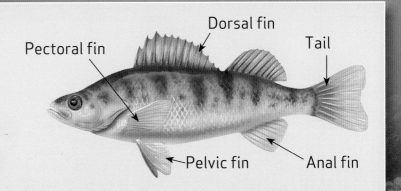

Dorsal fin

Pectoral fin

Tail

Pelvic fin

Anal fin

Living in a group

Many types of fish swim together in large groups called shoals. It is safer for fish to swim in shoals, because hunters can easily get confused by all the fish darting around.

A manta ray's wings can measure seven metres across.

Flying underwater

A manta ray looks a bit like a huge plane underwater. Its fins extend from its body to create enormous wings. The ray swims by flapping these wings to 'fly' through the water.

Lakes and Ponds

The water in ponds and lakes is called still water, because it hardly moves. Animals living there do not have to swim against a flow of water as they do in streams and rivers.

Plant life

Plants, such as reeds, grow in the shallow water around the edges of lakes and ponds. Many animals like to hide among the plant stems and eat the leaves.

Newts

Newts belong to a group of animals called amphibians. They spend most of their time swimming in the water, but they also have legs, so that they can walk across land.

This newt is brightly coloured to warn other animals that it is poisonous.

Freshwater fish

Many different kinds of fish are found in ponds and lakes, including this cichlid. Some fish feed on plants, while others hunt and eat other animals.

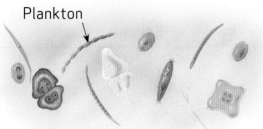

Plankton

Microscopic life

Pond water is full of tiny living things that are too small for us to see. These are called plankton and they include small plants, larvae (baby insects) and fish eggs.

Dragonfly larvae spend the first year of their lives in the water hunting other animals.

Dragonfly larvae

Dragonflies lay their eggs in water. The young that hatch from the eggs are called larvae. When the larvae become adults, they leave the water and fly away.

The Salmon

Salmon spend the first part of their lives in rivers. Then they travel to the sea, where they live for the next few years, feeding on fish and shellfish. After this, they make a long journey back to the river where they were born.

Powerful fish

Salmon are large, powerful fish. Their bodies are long and slim, which is ideal for swimming, and they have strong muscles to push them through the water.

Salmon swim by flicking their tails from side to side.

Salmon facts

🐾 Salmon live in both the Atlantic and Pacific Oceans.

🐾 The main types of salmon are the Atlantic, sockeye, chinook, pink, chum, coho and cherry salmon.

🐾 Sockeye salmon may swim more than 1500 kilometres from the Pacific Ocean to the rivers where they lay their eggs.

With a powerful flick of its tail, a salmon jumps up a waterfall.

Did you know?

The largest salmon is the chinook, or king, salmon. It can grow to more than 1.5 metres long and weigh up to 57 kilograms – almost as much as an adult human.

A feast of salmon

As the salmon swim up rivers and streams, other animals hunt them. Grizzly bears wait in the shallow parts of the rivers and use their strong jaws to catch the salmon as they swim past.

Heading up the river

Salmon spend most of their lives in the ocean. However, they have to lay their eggs in streams. Every year, millions of adult salmon swim into rivers, against the flow of the water. The journey is long and tiring and the salmon have to get over many obstacles, including waterfalls.

Farming salmon

People build special farms where they raise salmon to eat. The fish are kept in large floating cages, like the ones above, for up to 18 months.

Frogs and Toads

Frogs and toads belong to a group of animals called amphibians, which lay their eggs in water. Tadpoles hatch out of these eggs and change their shape as they grow into adults.

Frogspawn

A female frog lays about 100 eggs, which stick together in a clump called frogspawn. Each egg contains a tiny black dot that grows into a tadpole.

Frogspawn

Toads

Toads look very much like frogs, but there are a few differences. For example, toads usually have a warty skin, while frogs' skin is smooth.

Adult frogs

The froglets grow into adult frogs. Adults have large eyes and wide mouths, plus powerful back legs.

Froglet

Froglets

The tadpoles then grow front legs and their tails start to shrink. They are now called froglets, and they are ready to leave the water.

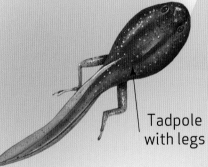

Tadpole with legs

Tadpoles

Growing legs

The tadpoles grow larger very quickly. About eight weeks after hatching, they have grown back legs.

Young tadpoles

Tadpoles have long tails but no legs. They breathe using gills, just like a fish.

Rivers

Animals that live in rivers have to cope with flowing water. Rivers also carry small pieces of mud and stones, which can make it difficult to see underwater.

River life

The mud on a riverbed is very good for plants to grow. The plants attract insects and other small animals to the rivers. These small creatures attract larger animals, such as fish and birds.

Female trout dig small nests in the gravel on riverbeds, where they lay their eggs.

Trout

The trout is a type of fish that loves fast-flowing water in streams and rivers. Its skin is brown and spotted, which helps it to hide among the mud and stones of a riverbed.

A dragonfly's huge eyes let the insect see right around its body.

River insects

Dragonflies are active hunters along river banks, catching insects while in flight. Other insects that live near rivers include damselflies and mayflies, which lay their eggs in the water.

Did you know?

Electric eels live in the rivers of South America. One electric eel produces enough electricity to power 12 light bulbs. Electric eels use this electricity to stun prey.

River birds

Swans and ducks are common along rivers, eating plants that grow on river banks or in the water. Swans build large nests on the river bank to raise their young, which are called cygnets.

Black swans live in southern Australia.

Estuaries

Estuaries are places where rivers flow into the sea. They are large, flat areas with lots of mud that small animals can burrow into.

River deltas

When a river reaches an estuary, it slows down and drops the mud it was carrying. This mud builds up to form a large, triangle-shaped area called a delta.

The Nile Delta forms where the river meets the Mediterranean.

River Nile

Cormorants can dive down to depths of 45 metres.

Did you know?

Some kinds of shore crab can run at up to 16 kilometres per hour.

Fish divers

Cormorants live alongside rivers, lakes, estuaries and seashores. They dive into the water to catch fish to eat. Some cormorants have even been trained to catch fish for humans.

Ragworms

A ragworm digs a U-shaped burrow into the mud. It then shoots its long jaws out of this burrow to catch and eat any small animal that gets too near.

Ragworms have flat bodies covered in bristles.

Beach hunters

Shore crabs are found on the mud of estuaries, the seashore and small streams. They feed on other animals that live in the mud, such as worms.

Shore crabs burrow into the mud to escape from birds.

Cockles

Cockles are bivalves. This means that they have two shells that are joined together. They dig into the mud when the tide is out, then they come out to feed when the tide comes in and they are covered by water.

Wading Birds

Estuaries attract large flocks, or groups, of birds. This is because the mud is full of small animals that birds love to eat. Each kind of bird has a different shape of beak for catching different animals.

Whimbrel

Whimbrels have long, curved beaks. They push their beaks into the mud to find worms, shrimps and crabs.

Long legs

Many of the birds found at estuaries, such as flamingos, have very long legs. They use these long legs to wade, or walk, through the water, looking for food.

Spearing fish

The heron has a long, pointed beak. It stands in the water and does not move. Once it spots a fish, it darts its head quickly forwards and catches the fish in its beak.

Oystercatchers

The oystercatcher has a strong, orange-red beak. It uses this to force open the closed shells of cockles and mussels to reach the animals inside.

Herons stand with their necks bent into an S-shape.

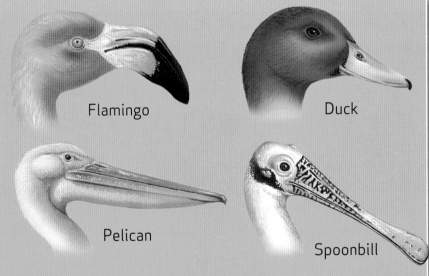

Flamingo

Duck

Pelican

Spoonbill

Beak shapes

Flamingos use their bent beaks to strain tiny animals out of the water. Ducks have a flat beak that can strain animals out of the mud. Pelicans have large pouches under their beaks, which they use to catch fish. Spoonbills have spoon-shaped beaks for scooping up animals from the mud.

Rocky Shores

Many shores are covered in rocks that have broken off cliffs. These rocks create pools and plenty of places for small animals to hide in when the tide goes out.

Changing tides

Twice a day, the sea rises up the shore and then goes out again. These movements are called tides. Because of the changing tides, animals on the shore are only underwater some of the time.

A starfish has suckers under each arm, which it uses for walking.

Starfish

The starfish is a hunter that eats mussels. It drills a hole in the mussel's shell to reach the animal inside.

Limpets

Limpets are small animals with hard shells. They hide inside their shells when the tide goes out. If, when the tide comes in, there is strong wave action, limpets use their muscular foot to cling very tightly to the hard surface on which they live.

Blennies eat small plants and animals, called plankton, which live in the water.

Walking fish

Blennies are small fish that are found in shallow water along the shore. They use their fins like feet and 'walk' under rocks to shelter from the crashing waves.

Rock Pools

Small pools of water are left between the rocks when the tide goes out. Lots of animals take shelter in these pools, waiting for the tide to return. These animals include sponges, urchins, crabs and small fish.

Did you know?

When a hermit crab grows bigger, it has to find a new, larger shell to live in.

Sea anemones

Sea anemones catch prey by waving their tentacles, or arms, in the water. They can pull in their tentacles to stop them being damaged.

Anemones have stinging cells in their tentacles to stun prey before feeding.

Filter feeder

Sponges have tiny holes on their bodies, which they use instead of mouths for eating. They suck water through these holes and strain small animals out of the water.

Hermit crabs

Hermit crabs make their homes inside empty shells to protect themselves from hunters. The crabs sometimes have a sea anemone as a passenger for protection. This helps them to hide when on the seabed.

The spines of some sea urchins are tipped with poison.

Prickly customer

Sea urchins are ball-shaped animals that are covered in spines, which protect them from hunters. They move around on the seabed looking for bits of small plants to eat.

Sandy Beaches

Sandy beaches may look deserted, especially when the tide is out. But there are lots of animals hiding beneath the sand.

Looking empty

When the tide goes out, beach animals dig into the sand to hide from the sun, wind and any hunters. They come out of hiding when the tide comes back in.

Worms leave small piles of sand, called wormcasts, at the entrances to their burrows.

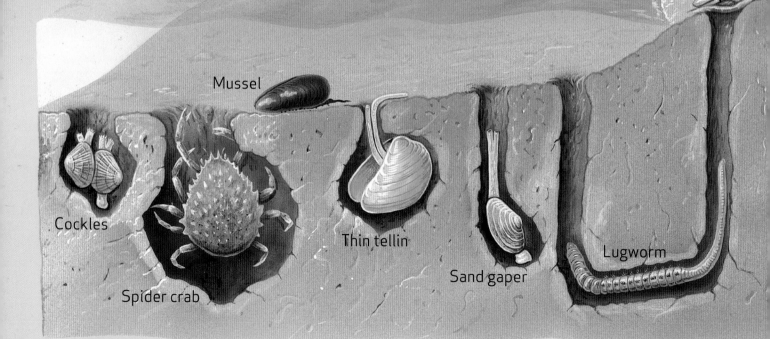

Mussel

Cockles

Spider crab

Thin tellin

Sand gaper

Lugworm

Sand dollar

The sand dollar is a type of
sea urchin. It lives just under
the surface of the beach,
where it digs through the
sand looking for food.

Mussels

Mussels live in large groups
on the beach. They attach
themselves to each other
and to the rocks using thin
strands called byssuses.

Razorshell

Kelp Forests

Kelp is a type of giant seaweed that grows in underwater forests. These are found in shallow water near the seashore. The huge seaweed forests provide shelter for fish and other sea creatures.

Inside the forest

Giant kelp can grow to 60 metres in length. It attaches itself to the seabed by roots called holdfasts. Thousands of fish swim between these massive blades of kelp, hiding from hunters, such as sharks.

Orange Garibaldis

The bright orange colour of the Garibaldi fish is a warning to other fish in the forest to stay away. Garibaldis are very aggressive fish and will even attack human divers!

Sea otters sometimes use rocks to smash open any shellfish.

Sea otters

Sea otters swim through the kelp looking for sea urchins to eat. They even sleep in the kelp forests, wrapping themselves up in kelp leaves so they do not float away.

Eagle rays

Eagle rays have an excellent sense of smell. They like to sniff out mussels and other shellfish, which they crunch up using their strong teeth.

The large wings on an eagle ray can measure more than two metres across.

Did you know?

Giant kelp is one of the fastest growing plants in the world. When conditions are good, kelp can grow more than 50 centimetres in a day!

Mangrove Swamps

Mangrove swamps are found along coasts near the Equator, which runs around the middle of the world. The water in these swamps is a mixture of salt water and fresh water. It is called brackish water.

Mangrove trees

The mangrove is an odd-looking tree. Its tangled roots act rather like stilts, holding the tree above the water.

Fiddler crabs are small, measuring just five centimetres across.

Waving claws

Male fiddler crabs have one claw that is much larger than the other. They use these huge claws to wave at and attract females.

Wading birds

Egrets wade through the swamp water on their long legs, using their feet to stir up mud on the bottom. This mud attracts small fish, frogs and insects, which the egrets catch and eat.

Land fish

The mudskipper is a type of fish that can move over land as well as through water. It 'walks' using its pectoral fins like little legs.

When the tide goes out, mudskippers move over land from pool to pool.

Did you know?

The Sundarbans in Bangladesh and India is the largest mangrove swamp in the world. It lies where the Ganges River flows into the Indian Ocean.

Coral Reefs

Coral reefs are some of the richest habitats in the world. They are home to millions of different creatures, including hunting sharks and enormous shellfish.

Skeleton home

Coral reefs are made by tiny creatures called coral polyps. Some of the polyps have a hard outer covering called a skeleton. When the polyps die, the skeletons are left behind and gradually build up to form the reef.

Coral polyps grow in lots of different shapes and colours.

Soft coral

Types of coral

There are two main types of coral polyp – hard coral and soft coral. Hard corals have a hard skeleton outside their bodies. Soft corals do not have a hard skeleton.

Hard coral

Reef hunters

Reef sharks are among the largest hunters on the reef. Some sharks swim in groups, called packs, looking for small fish to eat.

Giant clam

Giant clams

Giant clams are bivalves, meaning they have two shells that are joined together. These huge shellfish can grow to more than 1.5 metres across.

Reef Fish

Coral reefs are home to more than 4000 different kinds of fish. These fish feed on the millions of tiny plants and animals that live on the reefs.

Colourful groups

Anthias are a common reef fish. They swim together in large groups, or shoals, that can contain thousands of fish.

Parrotfish

Parrotfish are so named because their teeth are all at the front of their mouths and look like parrots' beaks.

Parrotfish use their beak-like teeth to scrape tiny plants called algae off the coral.

Beautiful but dangerous

The brightly coloured stripes of the lionfish
are a warning that this is a dangerous
creature. The fish's long spines contain
a poison that can kill other animals.

Living together

Anemones have stinging cells in
their tentacles, which can hurt
most fish. But clownfish can
live among the tentacles
because they are covered in
a slime that protects them
from the stings.

Open Ocean

The vast areas of open water between islands and continents are full of fish, whales, squid and other animals. Most of these animals are found near the water's surface, where there is plenty of sunlight.

Huge but harmless

The whale shark is a huge fish. It swims near the ocean's surface, using its enormous mouth to strain tiny animals from the sea water.

A whale shark's mouth is 1.5 metres wide.

Did you know?

Whale sharks are the largest fish swimming in the oceans. They often grow to more than nine metres long.

Whales are mammals
and need to come to the
water's surface to breathe.

Giant whales

The largest animals in
the oceans are the
whales. This is a beluga
whale. Even though belugas are
one of the smallest whales, they can still
grow to 4 metres long.

Cuttlefish

Cuttlefish belong to a group
of animals called molluscs.
They have eight short
tentacles and two long
tentacles that are
covered in suckers.

Cuttlefish use their
tentacles to pull food
into their mouths.

Sea turtles

Green sea turtles are
found in the warm waters
of the Atlantic, Pacific and
Indian Oceans. They feed
mainly on sea grasses and
small plants called algae.

Microscopic Life

Tiny animals called plankton float near the surface of the ocean. These animals are eaten by larger creatures, such as krill and fish. The krill and fish are themselves eaten by even larger animals, such as whales and dolphins. Without plankton, none of these animals would survive.

When they are large enough, crab larvae sink to the seabed and grow into adult crabs.

Young sea creatures

Plankton contains the larvae, or young, of many animals, including crabs. Crabs live on the seabed but their larvae float about in the water.

The bodies of baby fish are almost transparent, or see-through, to help hide them in the water.

Baby fish

Plankton also contains many types of young fish, including herring, eels and cod. These young fish hatch from eggs laid by adult fish.

Krill

Krill are pink, shrimp-like animals that are up to 15 centimetres long. They gather together in large groups called swarms. These swarms can be so big that they turn the water pink.

Some whales have baleen plates that are more than five metres long.

Plankton feeders

Many large whales feed on krill and plankton. They swallow water and strain out the tiny animals using long, bristly mouth plates, called baleen plates.

Did you know?

Female krill lay as many as 10,000 eggs at a time, several times a year.

Ocean Hunters

The ocean is not a safe place for a small animal because there are lots of hunters looking for their next meal. These hunters include birds flying above the surface, large fish such as barracudas, and mammals such as whales.

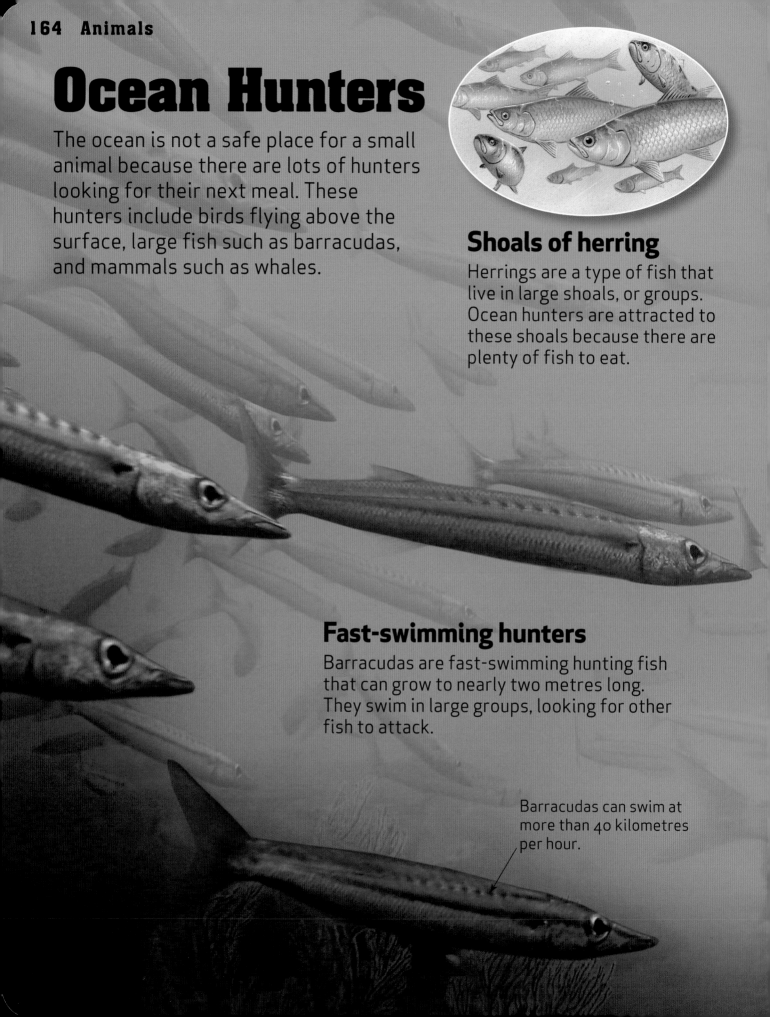

Shoals of herring

Herrings are a type of fish that live in large shoals, or groups. Ocean hunters are attracted to these shoals because there are plenty of fish to eat.

Fast-swimming hunters

Barracudas are fast-swimming hunting fish that can grow to nearly two metres long. They swim in large groups, looking for other fish to attack.

Barracudas can swim at more than 40 kilometres per hour.

Dive bombers

Pelicans fly over the ocean waiting for fish
to swim near the surface. Then they
dive into the water and
scoop up fish in the
pouches under
their beaks.

Sensitive sharks

Sharks have very good senses to detect prey.
They can smell a tiny drop of blood and can
feel the twitches made by an injured fish
from very far away.

Did you know?

Sharks have been
living in the
oceans for more
than 400 million
years.

Whales

Whales belong to a group of animals called mammals. They have to breathe air, just like humans. They do this through a nostril on top of the head, called a blowhole.

Breaching

Scientists do not know why whales leap out of the water in a move called breaching. It may be to attract a partner or to knock off other animals that are stuck to their bodies.

Like all mammals, baby whales feed on milk made by their mothers.

Baby whales

Instead of laying eggs, whales give birth to live babies. As soon as a baby whale is born, its mother pushes it to the surface to take its first breath of air.

Whale facts

- There are two main kinds of whale: toothed whales, which have teeth, and baleen whales, which have baleen plates instead of teeth, for straining food from water.

- A baby blue whale will drink up to 200 litres of milk from its mother every day – that is as much as 600 cans of lemonade.

Killer whales

Killer whales, also called orcas, live together in groups of up to 40 members. They hunt together as a group, looking for fish, birds, squid and even other whales to attack and eat.

Dolphins live in small groups called pods.

Dolphins

Dolphins are small whales. They have snouts that look like a beak. These snouts are filled with small teeth that are used to catch fish.

Did you know?

The world's biggest animal is the blue whale. It can grow to about 30 metres long.

Deep-sea Life

Sunlight cannot reach far below the ocean's surface. Down here, it is cold and dark, and there are very few creatures. Those animals that do live here have many ways of getting enough food to survive.

Viperfish

The viperfish has a mouth filled with long, sharp fangs. It uses these fangs to snatch prey and hold it firmly so that it does not escape.

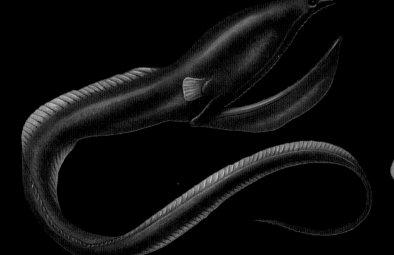

Gulper eel

The gulper eel has a huge mouth and stretchy stomach. This lets it swallow animals that are almost as big as itself.

Did you know?

Scientists have discovered a squid that is even larger than the giant squid. The colossal squid may grow up to 20 metres in length – that is longer than two buses.

Deep-sea giants

Sperm whales dive down to the deep ocean to hunt for their favourite food – giant squid. Some sperm whales have scars on their bodies from vicious fights with giant squid.

Giant squid grow to six to seven metres in length.

Gone fishing

The deep-sea anglerfish has a glowing bulb dangling over its mouth, which it uses to attract other fish. When the fish get too close, the anglerfish gobbles them up!

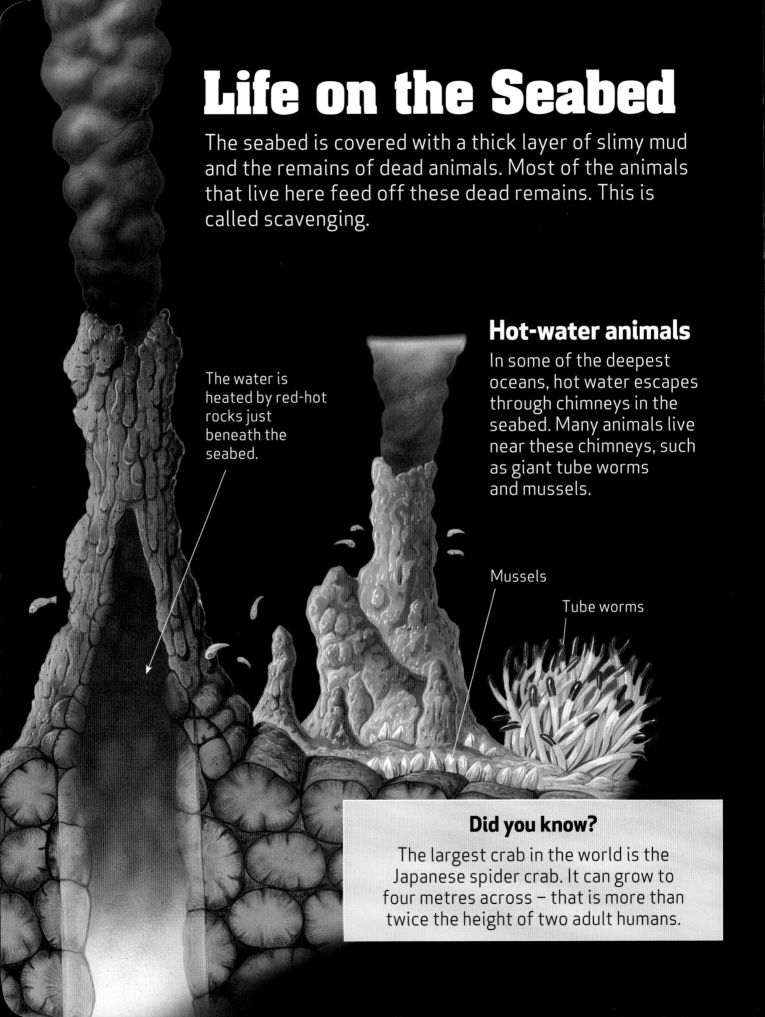

Life on the Seabed

The seabed is covered with a thick layer of slimy mud and the remains of dead animals. Most of the animals that live here feed off these dead remains. This is called scavenging.

The water is heated by red-hot rocks just beneath the seabed.

Hot-water animals

In some of the deepest oceans, hot water escapes through chimneys in the seabed. Many animals live near these chimneys, such as giant tube worms and mussels.

Mussels

Tube worms

Did you know?

The largest crab in the world is the Japanese spider crab. It can grow to four metres across – that is more than twice the height of two adult humans.

Grenadier fish

Grenadier fish have short bodies with long tails, and large mouths and eyes. They hunt for shellfish and other fish to eat, but they will also feed on dead bodies.

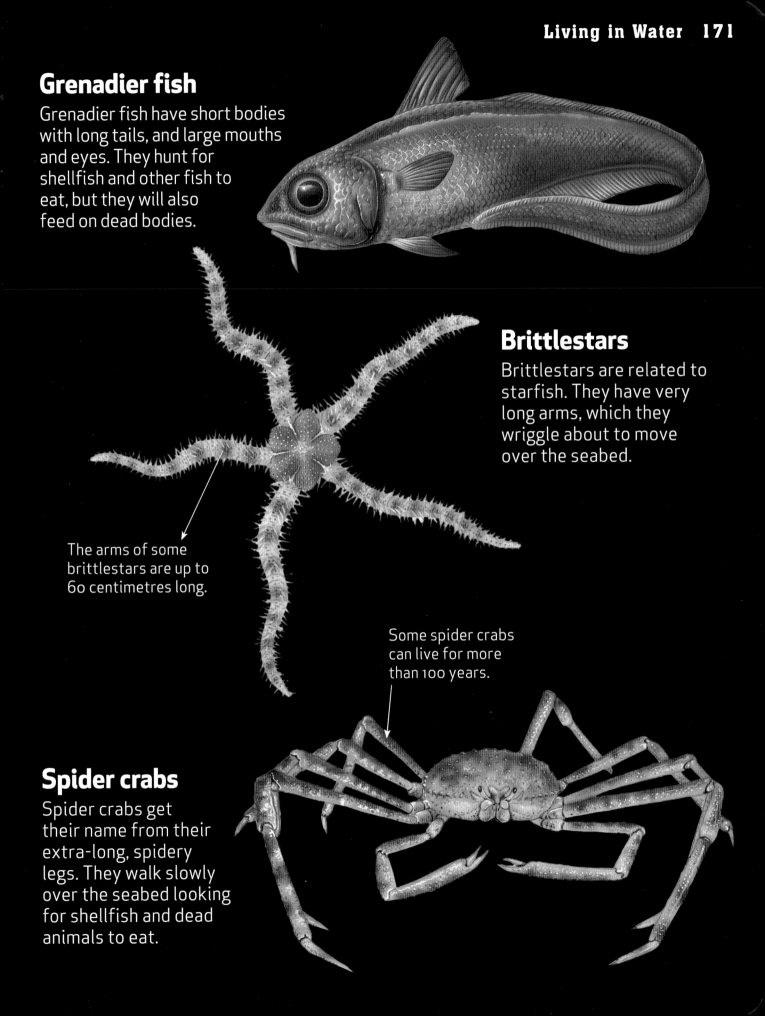

Brittlestars

Brittlestars are related to starfish. They have very long arms, which they wriggle about to move over the seabed.

The arms of some brittlestars are up to 60 centimetres long.

Some spider crabs can live for more than 100 years.

Spider crabs

Spider crabs get their name from their extra-long, spidery legs. They walk slowly over the seabed looking for shellfish and dead animals to eat.

INDEX

A

African wild dogs 47
alligators 24
amphibians 12, 16, 134, 138
angelfish 132
anglerfish 169
Antarctica 53, 89, 92–95
antelopes 20, 21, 60
anthias 158
ants 38, 39
Arctic 85, 86–87, 88
Arctic foxes 83
Arctic poppies 84
Arctic terns 89
arthropods 13
Atacama Desert 52

B

babies 11, 15, 17, 41, 63, 85
    90, 162, 166
    chicks 118–119
bacteria 21
badgers 62, 67
bald eagles 112–113
barracudas 164
bats 100, 120–123
beaches 150–151
bears 80–81, 86, 90–91, 137
bee-eaters 49
bees 96, 97, 125
beetles 51, 74
behaviour 14–15
bighorn sheep 104
bird watching 26
birds 108–119
    beaks 16, 33, 51, 87, 97,
    113, 145

chicks 118–119
eggs 11, 16, 93, 118–119
flightless 25, 114–115
forest 71, 73, 75, 79, 82–83
migration 77
nests 68, 71, 73, 75, 113,
116–117
river birds 141
skeleton 12
songbirds 35
waders 144–145, 155
wings 110–111
birds of prey 46, 47, 83, 108
birth 11
bison 64–65
bivalves 143, 157
blennies 147
blubber 86
blue jays 79
blue tits 73, 117
boas 30
body parts 12–13
breathing 10
brittlestars 171
brown bears 80–81
budding 17
buffalo 54
burrowing owls 67
butterflies 72, 96, 125,
126–127
buzzards 108

C

cacti 53
camels 58–59
camouflage 33, 36, 39, 75,
87, 90

canopy 30, 31, 32–33
caribou 88
carnivores 10, 21, 63
cassowaries 115
caterpillars 72, 73, 126–127
cave fish 101
cave spiders 101
caves 100–101
centipedes 13, 19
chameleons 32, 33
cheetahs 46, 47
chimpanzees 15
chinstrap penguins 93
chrysalis 127
cicadas 34
cichlids 135
cities 19, 98–99
climate change 23, 24, 25
clownfish 159
cockatoos 35
cockles 143, 145, 150
colossal squid 168
colonies 48, 94, 95
colour 14, 108
communication 14, 61,
    62, 105
conifers 78, 79
conservation 26–27
coral reefs 156–159
cormorants 114, 142
coyotes 61
crabs 13, 142, 143, 148, 149,
    150, 154, 162, 170, 171
crocodiles 24, 39, 43
cuckoos 118
cuttlefish 161

D E

deciduous trees 70
deer 76, 78, 85, 88
deltas 142
deserts 52–59
dinosaurs 24, 25
dodos 25
dolphins 22, 167
dormice 77
dragonflies 124, 135, 141
ducks 109, 145
dung beetles 51
eagles 102, 110, 112–113, 117, 119
earthworms 75
echolocation 122–123
eels 141, 162, 168
eggs
  birds 11, 16, 93, 118–119
  fish 162
  frogspawn 16, 138
  insects 49, 72, 73, 126, 135
egrets 155
elephants 17
emperor penguins 94
endangered animals 25, 26–27
epiphytes 31
estuaries 142–145
eucalyptus 68, 69
evergreen trees 70, 78
extinction 24–25
eyes 11, 123

F

falcons 99, 109
farm animals 96

farmland 96–97
fastest animals 47, 64, 114, 132, 164
feathers 14, 51, 82, 93, 94, 108, 109, 110, 111
feeding 10
ferrets 67
fins 132, 133
fish 12, 22
  freshwater 134–135, 140
  land fish 155
  reef fish 158–159
  sea 132–133, 152, 160–161, 164, 168, 169, 171
  shoals 15, 133, 164
  swimming 11, 132–133
fish farming 137
flamingos 144, 145
flowers 31, 53, 84, 97, 111
flying 107
  bats 120, 121
  birds 110–111
  insects 124–125
flying foxes 121
food chains 20–21
forests 19, 22, 68–79, 82–83, 102
  rainforests 23, 30–41
foxes 19, 54, 63, 87, 98
frogs 19, 35, 69, 138–139
frogspawn 16, 138
fruit bats 120, 121, 123
fur 87, 90

G

gall wasps 73
gannets 110
Garibaldi fish 152

geckos 55
geese 85
giant clams 157
giant pandas 25
giant squid 11, 168, 169
gibbons 37
giraffes 20, 44
global warming 23
goats 104, 105
golden eagles 102
goldfinches 97
gorillas 103
goshawks 83
grasslands 42–51, 60–67, 102
grazers 44–45
grenadier fish 171
gulls 110

H

habitats 18–19, 26, 29, 96, 102
  damage to 22–23
herbivores 10, 20
herds 63, 85
herons 10, 145
herring 162, 164
hibernation 77
horntails 79
houseflies 124
howler monkeys 34
human body 13
hummingbirds 111, 116
hunting 11, 15, 46–47, 61
  birds of prey 47
  in packs 46, 47, 61
  ocean hunters 164–165
hydras 17
hyenas 42

I J K

Icelandic cyprine 16
impalas 44
insects 13, 124–129
    eggs 49, 72, 73, 126, 135
    flying 124–125
    rainforests 33, 34, 38, 39
    woodland 72–73
invertebrates 12, 13
jackals 50
jaguars 39
jellyfish 12
katydids 33
kelp forests 152–153
kingfishers 108
kiwis 115
koalas 68, 69
krill 163

L M

ladybirds 125
lakes and ponds 19, 134–135
larvae 72, 126, 135, 162
leafcutter ants 38, 39
learning 14, 15
leopard seals 92
leopards 21, 46, 103
life cycles 16–17
limpets 147
lionfish 159
lions 14, 15, 21, 46
lizards 55, 56
llamas 63
locusts 54, 128–129
lugworms 150
lynx 79
macaws 33

mallards 109
mammals 12, 17, 166
    grasslands 62–63
mangrove swamps 154–155
marmots 105
meadows 96
meerkats 43
mice 19, 74, 77
migration 43, 77, 88–89
milk 17, 166
millipedes 70
moles 66, 67
molluscs 161
monkeys 34, 36, 37
moths 72, 126
mountains 18, 102–105
movement 11, 12, 36–37
mudskippers 155
mussels 145, 150, 151, 170

N O

national parks 25, 26
nest boxes 117
nests 48–49, 68, 71, 73, 75,
    113, 116–117
newts 134
oceans 18, 160–171
    deep sea life 168–169
    seabed 170–171
    shores 146–151
oil spills 23
omnivores 80
orang-utans 32
orcas 167
organic farming 27
organs, body 13
ostriches 114, 119
owls 11, 82, 111

oystercatchers 145

P R

pampas 60
parrotfish 158
peacocks 14
pelicans 145, 165
penguins 53, 92, 93, 94–95
pigeons 99
pigs 27
plankton 92, 135, 147,
    162, 163
plants 20, 31, 53, 84, 134
poison 57, 75, 134, 149, 159
polar bears 86, 90–91
porcupines 60, 61
prairie dogs 66, 67
prairies 60
predators 21, 46, 61
prehistoric animals 25
pronghorns 60
puffins 87
pupae 127
pythons 30
rabbits 10, 62, 63, 67
racoons 99
ragworms 143
rainforests 23, 30–39
rattlesnakes 57
rays 133, 153
razorshells 151
reindeer 85, 88
reproduction 16, 17
reptiles 11, 12, 56–57
rhinos 25
rivers 19, 140–141
rock pools 148–149
rocky shores 146–147

S

Sahara Desert 52
sailfish 132
salamanders 67
salmon 81, 136–137
sand dollars 151
sand dunes 52
sand gaper 150
savannahs 42–51
scavengers 50–51
scorpions 55
sea anemones 148, 159
sea birds 22, 23, 87, 165
sea otters 153
sea urchins 149, 151
seals 22, 53, 86, 92
seaweed 152–153
senses 10, 11, 122–123, 165
sequoias 71
sharks 157, 160, 165
sheep 17, 104
shells 13, 56, 143, 145, 147, 148, 149, 157
shoals 15, 133, 164
shores 146–151
sidewinders 57
sight 81, 83, 112
skeletons 12, 13, 156
skunks 77
sloths 36
slugs 19
snails 13, 19
snakes 19, 30, 37, 57, 67
snow geese 85
snow leopards 103
songbirds 35
sounds 14, 34–35, 61, 125

spider crabs 150, 171
spider monkeys 36, 37
spiders 13, 75, 101
sponges 149
spoonbills 145
squirrels 69, 76
stag beetles 74
starfish 146
steppes 60
storks 117
swallows 77, 110, 111, 116
swans 141
swarms 54, 128, 129, 163
swimming 11, 87, 91, 132–133

T

tadpoles 139
tails 36
tapirs 38, 39
teeth 40, 42, 71, 81
termites 15, 48–49
thin tellin 150
thorny devils 56
tides 146, 147, 150
tigers 25, 40–41
toads 16, 138
tool use 15
tortoises 24, 56
toucans 32
trees 22, 30–31, 42, 68–73, 154
    conifers 78, 79
    deciduous 70
    evergreen 70, 78
    largest 71
trout 140
tuna 132

tundra 84–85, 88
turkeys 83
turtles 161

V W

vampire bats 122, 123
vertebrates 12
viper fish 168
vultures 50, 51
wasps 73, 79
waterholes 45
weaver birds 117
webs 75, 101
whales 22, 53, 161, 163, 166–167, 169
whimbrels 144
wild boar 71
wildebeest 43, 46
wings
    bats 121
    birds 110–111
    insects 124–125, 129
winter 76–77, 78
wolf spiders 75
wolverines 84
wolves 14, 88
wombats 67
wood wasps 79
woodcocks 75
woodlice 19
woodpeckers 82
worms 75, 143, 150, 170
wrens 71

Y Z

yaks 105
zebras 43, 45
zoos 25, 41

Acknowledgments

All artwork supplied by Myke Taylor, The Art Agency

Photo credits:
b – bottom, t – top, r – right, l – left, m – middle

Front cover: all images sourced from Shutterstock and iStock apart from tiger: Getty Images/Darryl Estrine, elephant: Getty Images/Brad Wilson
Back cover: l Shutterstock, tr iStock, br iStock, m Stocktrek Images/Corey Ford

1 Dreamstime.com/David Davis, 2 Dreamstime.com/Harald Bolten, 3 Dreamstime.com, 4t Dreamstime.com/Richard Gunion, 5br Dreamstime.com/Asther Lau Choon Siew, 6tl Dreamstime.com/Kiyoshi Takahase Segundo, 6tr Dreamstime.com/Fred Goldstein, 6ml Dreamstime.com/Carolyne Pehora, 6-7m Digital Vision, 6t Dreamstime.com/Ian Scott, 7tr Dreamstime.com/Sanja Stepanovic, 7b Dreamstime.com/Wei Send Chen, 8-9 Corbis/Gallo Images, 10bl Dreamstime.com/Johannes Gerhardus Swanepoel, 11tr Dreamstime.com/Vaida Petreikiene, 11m Dreamstime.com, 11b Dreamstime.com/Stephen Inglis, 12br Dreamstime.com, 12-13 Dreamstime.com/Andre Nantel, 13t Dreamstime.com/Radu Razvan, 13m Dreamstime.com/Vladimir Ivanov, 14tl Dreamstime.com, 14b Dreamstime.com/Mark Karasek, 15tr Dreamstime.com/Vladimir Kindrachov, 15b Dreamstime.com, 16t Dreamstime.com/Tomas Hajek, 16b Dreamstime.com, 17m Dreamstime.com, 17b Dreamstime.com/Steffen Foerster, 18 Dreamstime.com/Stuart Elflett, 18b Dreamstime.com/George Bailey, 19t Dreamstime.com/Bartlomiej Kwieciszewski, 19m Dreamstime.com, 19b Dreamstime.com, 20m Dreamstime.com/Anna Kowalska, 20bl Dreamstime.com, 21br Dreamstime.com, 22t Dreamstime.com/David Hyde, 22b Digital Vision, 23t Digital Vision, 23b Digital Vision, 24 Dreamstime.com/Fah mun Kwan, 25br Dreamstime.com/Nico Smit, 26tr Dreamstime.com/Steven Pike, 26b Dreamstime.com/Steffen Foerster, 27t Digital Vision, 27b Dreamstime.com/John Bloor, 28–29 Corbis/Kennan Ward, 30t Tall Tree Ltd, 30b Dreamstime.com, 31t Tall Tree Ltd, 31m Dreamstime.com, 32tl Dreamstime.com/Phil Date, 32br Dreamstime.com/Kathy Wynn, 33tr Dreamstime.com , 33m Tall Tree Ltd, 33b Dreamstime.com/Michael Ledray, 34tl Dreamstime.com, 34br Dreamstime.com/Christopher Marin, 35t Dreamstime.com/David Davis, 35b Dreamstime.com, 36–37 Dreamstime.com, 37br Dreamstime.com, 38t Tall Tree Ltd, 38b Dreamstime.com/Mike Evans, 39t Dreamstime.com/Ferenc Cegledi, 39b Dreamstime.com, 40b Dreamstime.com, 41tr Dreamstime.com/Graça Victoria, 41m Dreamstime.com/Tze Roung Tan, 42–43 Dreamstime.com/Stefan Ekernas, 42bl Dreamstime.com, 43m Digital Vision, 43r Dreamstime.com, 44b Dreamstime.com/Andre Maritz, 44–45 Dreamstime.com, 45t Dreamstime.com, 45br Dreamstime.com/Steffen Foerster, 46–47 Corbis, 46b Digital Vision, 47tr Dreamstime.com, 47br Dreamstime.com, 48tl Dreamstime.com/Michael Pettigrew, 48–49 Dreamstime.com/Craig Ruaux, 49r Digital Vision, 50-51 Dreamstime.com/Chris Fourie, 50b Dreamstime.com/Steve Meyfroidt, 51t Dreamstime.com, 51b Dreamstime.com/Laura Frankel, 52–53 Dreamstime.com/Vladimir Pomortsev, 52b Dreamstime.com/Michael Schofield, 53t Dreamstime.com, 53b Dreamstime.com/Alexander Putyata, 54tl Dreamstime.com/Steve Schowiak, 54b Dreamstime.com/Vladimir Pomortsev, 55t Dreamstime.com, 55b Digital Vision, 56-57 Dreamstime.com, 57t Dreamstime.com/Stephen McSweeny, 58 Dreamstime.com/Dario Diament, 59t Dreamstime.com/Julija Mezecka, 59b Dreamstime.com/Keith Naylor, 60–61 Dreamstime.com/Tyler Olson, 60b Dreamstime.com/Michael West, 61b Dreamstime.com/Ken Griffith, 62t Digital Vision, 62b Dreamstime.com/Joe Gough, 63t Dreamstime.com, 63b Dreamstime.com/Andreas Steinbach, 64–65 Dreamstime.com, 65t Dreamstime.com, 65br Dreamstime.com, 66tl Dreamstime.com/Bob Wolverton, 67m Dreamstime.com/Gary Unwin, 67b Dreamstime.com/Pavel Gribkov, 68 tl Dreamstime.com, 68br Dreamstime.com, 69t Dreamstime.com, 69b Dreamstime.com/Ruta Saulyte-Laurinaviciene, 70tl Digital Vision, 70bl Digital Vision, 71t Dreamstime.com/Robert Hambley, 71b Dreamstime.com/Jorge Felix Costa, 72t Dreamstime.com/Martina Berg, 72b Dreamstime.com/Gumenuk Vitalij, 73 Dreamstime.com/Edite Artmann, 74tl Dreamstime.com/Gumenuk Vitalij, 74br Dreamstime.com, 75t Dreamstime.com/Michael Pettigrew, 75b Corbis/Roger Tidman, 76tr Dreamstime.com, 76b Dreamstime.com/Bruce Macqueen, 77tr Dreamstime.com, 77br Dreamstime.com, 78b Dreamstime.com/Tony Campbell, 79t Digital Vision, 79mr Dreamstime.com/Robert Hambley, 79br Dreamstime.com, 80 Dreamstime.com, 81 Dreamstime.com/Ryhor Zasinets, 82tl Dreamstime.com, 82br Dreamstime.com, 83tl Dreamstime.com/Bruce Macqueen, 83br Dreamstime.com, 84tl Dreamstime.com/Sergey Anatolievich, 84m Dreamstime.com/Gail Johnson, 84bl Dreamstime.com/Sergey Anatolievich, 85t Dreamstime.com/Aaron Whitney, 85b Dreamstime.com/Maggie Dziadkiewicz, 86t Dreamstime.com/Anthony Hathaway, 86b Dreamstime.com/Steffen Foerster, 87t Dreamstime.com, 87b Dreamstime.com/Holger Wulschlaeger, 88bl Dreamstime.com/Geoffrey Kuchera, 88–89 Dreamstime.com/Lauren Jones, 89t Dreamstime.com/Roy Longmuir, 90 Dreamstime.com/Carolyne Pehora, 91t Dreamstime.com/Anthony Hathaway, 91b Dreamstime.com/Kathleen Struckle, 92t Dreamstime.com/Alexander Putyata, 92b Dreamstime.com/Jan Will, 92t Dreamstime.com/Alexander Putyata, 92b Dreamstime.com/Bernard Breton, 94b Dreamstime.com/Bernard Breton, 95t Dreamstime.com/Bernard Breton, 95b Dreamstime.com/Neil Wigmore, 97t Dreamstime.com/Peter Mautsch, 96bl Dreamstime.com/Martina Berg, 96br Dreamstime.com, 97tr Dreamstime.com/Richard McDowell, 97bl Dreamstime.com/Marilyn Barbone, 98t Tall Tree Ltd, 98b Dreamstime.com/Nicola Gavin, 99t Dreamstime.com/Xavier Marchant, 99ml Dreamstime.com/Wael Hamdan, 99br Dreamstime.com/Piotr Bieniecki, 100 Dreamstime.com, 101br Corbis/DK Limited, 102m Dreamstime.com/Glen Gaffney, 102b Dreamstime.com, 103tl Dreamstime.com/Mike Carlson, 103br Dreamstime.com/Vladimir Pomortsev, 104 Dreamstime.com/Rick Parsons, 105tl Dreamstime.com/Keith Yong, 105tr Dreamstime.com/Kaleb Timberlake, 105br Dreamstime.com/Sascha Burkard, 106-107 Corbis/Steve Kaufman, 108bl Digital Vision, 108m Digital Vision, 109t Dreamstime.com, 109b Dreamstime.com/John Sfondilias, 110 Digital Vision, 111tr Dreamstime.com/Willie Manalo, 111tl Digital Vision, 111br Dreamstime.com/Kiyoshi Takahase Segundo, 112t Dreamstime.com/Robert Cocquyt, 113t Dreamstime.com/Matt Ragen, 113b Dreamstime.com/Stephen Inglis, 114t Digital Vision, 114b Dreamstime.com/Roy Longmuir, 115br Dreamstime.com/Linda Bucklin, 116tl Digital Vision, 116b Dreamstime.com/Ivan Chuyev, 117tl Dreamstime.com/Vaida Petreikiene, 117br Digital Vision, 118m Dreamstime.com/Scott Impink, 118bl Dreamstime.com/Johannes Gerhardus Swanepoel, 119tr Digital Vision, 119b Digital Vision, 120 Corbis, 121tr Dreamstime.com/Angela Farley, 121ml Dreamstime.com, 121bl Dreamstime.com/Paul Cowan, 122tl Dreamstime.com/Geza Farkas, 123 Dreamstime.com/Adam Booth, 124tr Digital Vision, 124b Dreamstime.com/Bobby Deal, 125tr Dreamstime.com/Fred Goldstein, 126br Dreamstime.com/Sanja Stepanovic, 126-127 Dreamstime.com/Elaine Davis, 126b Dreamstime.com, 127b Dreamstime.com/Geza Farkas, 128tr Dreamstime.com/Nico Smit, 129r Dreamstime.com/Alice Dehaven, 130–131 Corbis/Jeffrey L. Rotman, 132m Dreamstime.com/Ellen McIlroy, 133r Digital Vision, 133b Dreamstime.com, 134t Dreamstime.com/Mike Brake, 134b Dreamstime.com/Michael L., 135t Dreamstime.com/Dallas Powell, jr., 135b Dreamstime.com, 103tl Dreamstime.com/Holger Leyrer, 136b Dreamstime.com/Daniel Slocum, 137t Dreamstime.com/Michael Thompson, 137b Dreamstime.com/David Hyde, 138–139 Dreamstime.com/Andrei Contiu, 138b Dreamstime.com/Bruce MacQueen, 140t Dreamstime.com/Chris Schlosser, 140b Corbis/Dale C. Spartas, 141tl Dreamstime.com/Richard Merwin, 141b Digital Vision, 142 tl NASA, 142bl Dreamstime.com/Anita Huszti, 143m Dreamstime.com/Sergey Khachatryan, 143br Dreamstime.com/Joseph Helfenberger, 144tr Dreamstime.com/Caroline Henri, 144b Digital Vision, 145tl Dreamstime.com/Stefan Ekernas, 145br Dreamstime.com/Christina Craft, 146 iStockphoto.com, 146b Dreamstime.com/Jamie Wilson, 147t Dreamstime.com/Stuart Key, 147b Dreamstime.com/Uwe Ohse, 148 Dreamstime.com, 149tr Dreamstime.com/Asther Lau Choon Siew, 149ml Dreamstime.com/Asther Lau Choon Siew, 149br Dreamstime.com/Daniela Spyropoulou, 151t Dreamstime.com, 151br Dreamstime.com/Jay Prescott, 152t Dreamstime.com/Jeff Waibel, 152b Dreamstime.com, 153tr Dreamstime.com, 153br Dreamstime.com, 154t Dreamstime.com/Daniel Gustavsson, 154b Dreamstime.com/Anthony Hall, 155r Dreamstime.com/Humberto Ortega, 156–157 Dreamstime.com/Matthias Weinrich, 156bl Dreamstime.com/Asther Lau Choon Siew, 156br Dreamstime.com/Asther Lau Choon Siew, 157t Dreamstime.com/Ian Scott, 157b Dreamstime.com/Asther Lau Choon Siew, 158t Dreamstime.com/Asther Lau Choon Siew, 158b Dreamstime.com/Ian Scott, 159m Dreamstime.com/Wei Send Chen, 159b Dreamstime.com/Andrea Leone, 160t Dreamstime.com/Harald Bolten, 161t Dreamstime.com/Jeremy Bruskotter, 161m Dreamstime.com, 161b Dreamstime.com, 163b Corbis, 164 Dreamstime.com/Asther Lau Choon Siew, 165t Dreamstime.com/Steve Weaver, 165b Dreamstime.com/Ian Scott, 166–167 Dreamstime.com/Brett Atkins, 167t Dreamstime.com/Jason Vandehey, 167br Digital Vision